A
Northampton
Childhood
in the 1960s

A Northampton Childhood
in the 1960s

Christine Jones

AMBERLEY

First published 2014

Amberley Publishing
The Hill, Stroud
Gloucestershire
GL5 4EP

www.amberleybooks.com

. British Library Cataloguing in Publication Data.
A catalogue record for this book is available from the British Library.

ISBN 978 1 4456 2150 0 (print)
ISBN 978 1 4456 2156 2 (ebook)

Typesetting and Origination by Amberley Publishing.
Printed in Great Britain.

Contents

One	My First Home	7
Two	Grandma	14
Three	The Shop	22
Four	Time With Auntie	29
Five	Primary School	48
Six	Growing Up	59
Seven	A New Home	68
Eight	Kerr Street	78
Nine	Leisure Time	89
Ten	Senior School	110
Eleven	Changing Times	120
	Acknowledgements	127

Chapter One

My First Home

My earliest memories are not filed away tidily in my mind like photographs in an album. They are more haphazard, like the dog-eared photographs crammed into my grandmother's shoebox, ready to tumble out and jostle for attention as soon as the string is untied – treasured fragments of memory and tantalising glimpses through the window of time. I was born in 1961, a time when the world was changing very quickly. My first home was a large and comfortable flat above my father's newsagent's shop in St James Road. I lived there with my parents and my paternal grandmother. My parents were modern, forward-looking and full of energy, while my grandma was my link to the past.

When I was born, an extra bedroom was needed, so my parents made plans for the flat to be extended and for the shop to be modernised. I only have vague memories of the work being done, but I remember being so impressed by an apprentice builder called Jim that I wanted to be a builder when I grew up. Our flat had a big front room with a bay window, which looked down on to St James Road. There was as a deep ledge like a bench below the window and I could sit there and watch the world going by. There was a hall between the front room and the dining room; on one side there was a door where the original stairs from the shop once led up to the flat, but after the alterations it was just a cupboard. Next to the cupboard were the stairs, which led up to the bedrooms, and the bathroom was on the other side of the hall opposite.

The dining room was a comfortable room with a window that looked out at St James church tower; a view that became almost as familiar to me as looking in the mirror. The kitchen window looked out across our little roof garden and across the back of the houses in Althorp Road in the direction of Victoria Park. When I was out playing on the flat roof, I could hear the happy hubbub of playground noises and I could look over and see the children in the playground at St James School. My bedroom also looked out across the rooftops at the back, but it was the sounds that I loved more than the view. We were close enough to Castle station to hear the trains and at night, when I went to bed, I listened to the familiar railway sounds. There was a fireplace in my bedroom, but I don't remember ever having an open fire in my room. We had night storage heaters and I don't remember ever feeling cold.

My parents before I was born.

Me with my mum in Wales, June 1963.

The big bay window in our front room was my window on the world. As a very young child, I remember being held up to look out of the window and see the milkman's horse go past in the morning. That was the only horse and cart that I can remember among the busy main road traffic, and I expect it was soon replaced by a more modern means of milk delivery. I'm told that the rag-and-bone man also had a horse and cart, but for some reason I can only recall a handcart. I remember him shouting out as he walked along – we could often hear him shouting as he walked around the nearby streets. I couldn't understand what he was shouting – it didn't sound like words at all – but the adults understood. Apparently, he was saying, 'Old rags are lovely.'

St James Road was busy and there was always something for me to see as I looked down from my window. There was a bus stop almost outside and I could observe the people waiting for the bus to take them into town. The big, red Corporation buses came past every few minutes, so the noise of their engines and the 'ding ding' of the

Castle station, Northampton. (*Copyright John Evans*)

conductor's bell were as familiar to me as the sound of my own breathing. My parents had a car, but I sometimes travelled into town on the bus with my mum when she went shopping or went to have her hair done at the John London salon on the Drapery.

There were always people coming and going, people on their way to or from work. The Mettoy factory was close by on Harlestone Road, and Church's shoe factory was on the other side of St James Road, close to the Corporation bus depot. Express Lifts was just a short walk along the Weedon Road and British Timpkin was not far away in Duston. I liked to watch the children going to and from St James School, which was next to the church, very close to my home. Some of the younger ones walked with their mothers, but most of the children walked to school on their own or with an older sibling.

If I looked across the road, I could see Mr Green's chemist shop on the corner of Alma Street. I sometimes went there with my mother but I didn't like it very much. Mr Green seemed very old, he was always kind, but I didn't like the things we bought from the chemist. My mother bought rosehip syrup, which had to be diluted with water, and I was given some to drink every day because it was good for me. I wasn't very keen on it, but it wasn't as bad as Minadex, a sticky, orange-flavoured tonic, which I detested – I had to take that every day too. If my gums were sore, a tincture of myrrh was dabbed onto them to ease the pain and if I had toothache, my grandmother would give me a clove to hold in my mouth near the tooth. I'm not sure if the clove helped, but it tasted nice. When I had coughs and colds, camphorated oil was rubbed on my chest to ease my breathing; it smelled horrible. Beyond the chemist was Golby's florist shop and a small electrical shop, run by Mr Barton. I occasionally went to the florist with my mum but I don't remember going to Mr Barton's shop. He had a daughter who was about the same age as me and we sometimes played together.

The post office was directly across the road and next to it (on the Weedon Road side) there were a couple of houses and then a pub called the West End Tramcar. Then there was a little road – Abbey Street, I think – and then a police box and a couple more shops: Mitchell's the butcher, and Gunthorpe's, which I think was a greengrocer's shop. I don't remember ever being taken to the post office or to the two little shops near the police box. We did, however, go to Adams, the baker's shop on the opposite corner of Weedon Road, to buy our bread. The Northampton Town and County Building Society was on the corner of Harlestone Road, where we sometimes went to pay money into my savings account. I had a savings box in the shape of a book and when it was full of shillings, two shillings and half crowns, we took it to be emptied. A little further along the Harlestone Road was St Andrew's Methodist church. This was the church that my family attended, but I didn't like it very much and I detested Sunday school.

The Mettoy Factory was on the opposite side of Harlestone Road. A little further down, closer to the junction with Althorp Road, was the Co-op, Strikes the greengrocer's and Sketchley the dry cleaning shop. My grandma bought our groceries from Strikes; she would take her big shopping bag and potatoes and vegetables would be tipped into her bag unwrapped, then fruit in brown paper bags would be carefully placed on top. Just around the corner, in Althorp Road, was a small butcher's shop run by Mr Vickers. For reasons lost in time, my grandma bought most of our meat from Mr

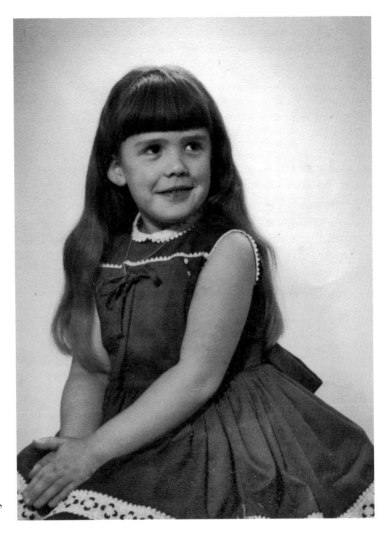

A photograph of me,
aged five or six.

Askew in Clare Street, but we sometimes called into the little shop to buy a pound and
a half of the best pork sausages from Mr Vickers. When you crossed Althorp Road,
you came to St James Road. The National Westminster bank was on the corner and
then there was another small butcher's shop, which belonged to Mr Lewis. Next, there
was the entrance to the library. It had a big wooden door and steep steps, which led
up to the books. It was one of my favourite places and I can still remember the sounds
and smells of St James Library. Next came my dad's newsagent's shop, then Baxter's
the butcher's and Worthington's the grocer's; after that was the school playground and
then the church.

My world was limited by the main road. I rarely crossed the road except to go to the
chemist with my mum, to go to Sunday school at Harlestone Road Methodist church or
to accompany one of my parents on a paper round if one of the paper boys didn't turn up.
I was more familiar with the roads on our side of the main road. I would often go with my

Grandma to Strikes the greengrocer's, and we would occasionally go to Worthington's to buy one or two grocery items. We had meat delivered every week and I think we must have had groceries delivered too – we certainly didn't go to the supermarket.

My father rented a garage in Orchard Street from a man called Fred Richardson. I often used to walk round to the garage with my dad to get the car. The outer doors to the garage led under an archway, which had a building above it. Beyond the archway to the right, some steps led up to a door, which I think was Mr Richardson's workshop; in front of us was an open yard and across the yard were a couple of garages. Ours was on the left-hand side. We had a big white Chrysler with a bench seat at the front, so I usually sat between my parents when we went out in the car.

My parents took me to the library to choose new books every week. In those early days, I didn't know how lucky I was to live right next door to St James Library. It didn't look like a library from the outside, as all you could see was a tall, heavy door, but beyond the doors a flight of steps led up to the library. When you pushed open the door at the top of the stairs, you were greeted by a comfortable hush and the special library smell of wood, polish and books. The librarian was a lady called Anne Norman, who always wore her hair up in a severe style, but she had a ready smile and a sense of fun; I liked her and I liked the library. I was very attached to my old favourites and I took the same books home over and over again. Best of all were the Bobby Brewster books, about a young boy who had unusual adventures. My parents must have dreaded yet another evening with Bobby Brewster, but they read the stories with enthusiasm and I loved that warm feeling of cuddling up next to them with a favourite book.

I didn't mind going to the shops with my mum or my grandma, but I preferred going out for a walk. If one of the paper boys didn't turn up, one of my parents would have to do the round instead. This was extremely irritating for them but to me it was an adventure, a chance to walk around some of the streets that I didn't often see and an opportunity to chat to people on the way. Even if they were moaning about their newspapers being late, they were usually friendly and they always had a kind word for me. Going to Victoria Park was even better than going out on a paper round. I loved going to the park and I went there often. To me, it seemed that I was surrounded by family members who all loved to take me to the park, but in reality my parents had to work very hard and there were times when they relied on other people to look after me. My dad sometimes took me to the park but, oddly, I don't remember going to the park with my mum. Usually, I would be taken to the park by one of my grandmothers or my grown-up cousin, Carole. We walked along Althorp Road to get to there. On a nearby corner was a little shop that belonged to Mrs Hodges. She sold newspapers too, and we would often stop and have a little chat with her.

My grandmothers probably didn't enjoy our visits to the park as much as I did, because they always wanted to stop me doing the things that I really wanted to do. I was not allowed to paddle in the stream in case I cut my feet and I was warned not to go over the stepping stones in case I slipped and got my shoes wet. It was impossible to resist the temptation of the stepping stones, despite getting in trouble for spoiling my shoes. However, my favourite spot was not the playground or the lovely little stream with stepping stones – it was the special high bench in the far corner of the park. The

The trainspotting bench in Victoria Park. (*Copyright John Evans*)

bench enabled me to look across the river to the railway line, and I would sit there for ages watching trains.

In those days, there was much more traffic on the line; a child doing the same thing today would die of boredom! By then, steam was already a rarity, but I was just as happy to watch what my dad called the 'smelly old diesels'. I liked them and, even as a little girl, I was fascinated by freight trains. On Wednesdays and Saturdays, I used to walk across Westbridge on the way to my aunt's house in Albion Place. She would let me scramble up and look down over the wall at the station below, as there was always something to see. I loved the sounds and the smells of the railway. I still do, but the smells have more or less gone, and the sounds are different now.

Chapter Two

Grandma

My grandmother lived with us and I now realise that she made life very difficult for my parents, but very little of the tension and frustration was noticeable to me at the time. I had no idea that she had not wanted a grandchild because she was jealous of her place in the family, and by the time I was old enough to notice, she had recovered from her deep disappointment that I was not a boy. In her eyes, boys were superior because she had produced a son (my father), who was allegedly born potty trained, walking, talking and with impeccable manners! Despite her initial rejection, we grew to love each other and she had a massive influence on my life.

Grandma was born in 1891, and she had known real poverty in her childhood. Like many men of his day, her father drank and her mother struggled to raise her large family. As an adult, Grandma had lived through two world wars; three of her brothers died in the first war and another brother was injured. Then, like countless other mothers, she had to live with the fear of losing her precious son in the second war. By the time I arrived, she had been a widow for more than a decade and the loss of my grandfather, Mick, had left her with a deep and enduring sadness. Sometimes I would go with her to tend his grave at Kingsthorpe cemetery. She called it 'grandpa's little garden'. Much more often, I would curl up on her bed eating a finger of her special Callard and Bowsers dessert nougat while she told me stories about him. Through her memories, my grandfather and grandma's whole family became far more than names. They are still as real to me as if I had actually known them.

Food rationing had finally ended in 1954 and when I arrived in the early 1960s, I was given the best of everything to make me 'big and strong'. I was given rich and creamy gold-top milk because it was good for me – how times have changed! Needless to say, my baby photographs are deeply embarrassing. I looked like the Michelin Man's daughter!

My grandma would often tell me that a little of what you fancy does you good, and as she cooked, she would give me a handful of raisins or a little taste of whatever she was cooking. I liked it best of all when she baked cakes. I stood on a chair next to her and watched, fascinated, eager to be allowed to scrape the bowl when she had finished. Often she told me stories while she cooked. Sometimes it was about always being hungry when she was a little girl, about food rationing during the war or about

My grandparents, Mick and Ethel, *c.* 1948. My grandfather died before I was born.

starving children in other countries. She did her best to make me understand that there were still people who didn't have enough food. On Thursdays, it was half-closing day, so we could all eat together when the shop closed. My grandma always cooked fish and chips on Thursdays, and I stood on my chair watching as she dipped each piece of fish into raw egg and then into homemade breadcrumbs. When we had haddock, she showed me the black mark on the skin, which she said was put there to remind us of the thumbprint of Jesus and the way he blessed the five loaves and two fishes, so that there was enough food to feed 5,000 people.

Grandma had a big blue-and-white-striped jar, filled with lumps of cooking salt, and she would break off a piece to add to the saucepan when cooking vegetables. She never weighed anything, gauging the quantities needed by eye or with an old cup and spoon. She kept a chipped cup for measuring flour, sugar and other dry ingredients and another cup with a broken handle to break eggs into. She would never break an egg straight into the mixing bowl because a bad egg would spoil everything and she hated waste. Nothing was wasted. The meat left over from our Sunday roast was sliced and eaten cold with vegetables and gravy on Monday and any leftover meat was minced and used to make another meal. I loved that old mincer – a big, heavy thing that gripped the side of the table. I always wanted to turn the handle but I wasn't strong enough, so Grandma would put her hand over mine and we turned it together. Cooking in those days required strength and stamina; Grandma could beat the mixture by hand faster and for longer than I have ever managed. She used a little hand whisk with a turn handle to whisk egg whites, a job that I was sometimes trusted with but it took me much longer to achieve the stiff white peaks that she wanted.

We had some modern gadgets too. Grandma loved the Kenwood mixer, but she only used it if she was doing a lot of baking, otherwise she would get the mixing bowl out and do everything by hand. We had an automatic washing machine – a Hoover Keymatic. Thick, coloured plastic squares with notches in the edges pushed into a slot on the front of the machine, the notches representing different wash programs. That machine lasted right through my childhood. We had a drying rack on a pulley. When not in use, it was wound all the way up to the kitchen ceiling, but when there were damp garments to be dried it was let down, the garments were placed over the wooden poles and then it was pulled back up towards the ceiling. In the corner of the kitchen, there was a big Colston dishwasher. It was very noisy and a bit temperamental, so Grandma seemed to think that it was quicker and easier to do the washing up by hand.

The Bible played a big part in my grandma's life and she would often read stories to me from my big illustrated children's Bible. I liked the Old Testament stories best of all:

Me with my grandma.

Daniel in the lion's den, Moses in the bulrushes, David and Goliath and the parting of the Red Sea. My favourite was the story of God speaking to Samuel. Grandma's own Bible was kept by her bed. I was too young to read it, but I knew I wasn't going to like it because it was full of rules to stop us having fun. According to Grandma, it was wrong to play outside on a Sunday; I could walk in the park but I was not allowed to play on the swings. We couldn't sew or knit on a Sunday because it would make God unhappy and even the thought of playing cards on a Sunday was terribly wicked.

Unfortunately for my parents, Grandma had turned disapproval into a performing art and she could always quote a Bible verse to support her beliefs. When miniskirts became popular, Grandma was scandalised and she warned that it was as bad as Sodom and Gomorrah. When my mother wore a miniskirt, Grandma announced that she had lived too long and she would be glad when her time came. She disapproved of my mother's make-up too, telling me that the body was the temple of God and we should not put that muck on our faces. Just to be sure that I got the message, she told me that lipstick was made of beetle's blood. Grandma used face powder, but when my mum pointed out that powder was also make-up, Grandma was indignant; she insisted that it was not to make her look attractive, it was just to take the shine off her nose! Poor Mum – it must have been hard to keep her temper at times.

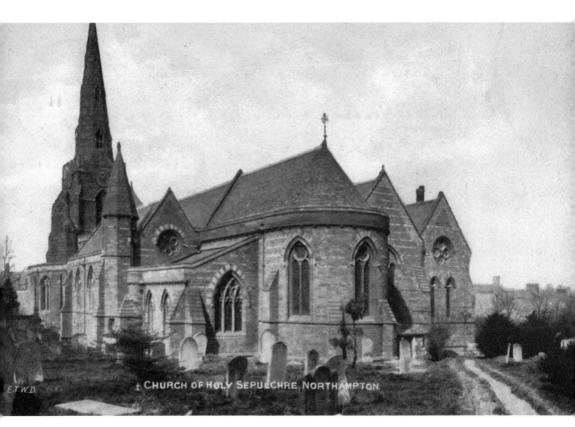

The church of the Holy Sepulchre as my grandma would have known it.

My mum and dad worked all day from Monday to Saturday and all morning on Sundays, so Grandma did some of the washing and ironing. She would sigh and mutter as she folded the underwear. Many of my mother's clothes caused comment from my grandmother, but none more than her pants, which, according to Grandma, were shamefully small and not even big enough to be cut up for dusters. They were what we would describe today as a full brief, but in comparison to Grandma's knee-length bloomers, they were skimpy. We were not poor, but old and worn-out undergarments were cut up and used as dusters, floor cloths or polishing cloths. Outgrown clothes were passed on and worn out clothes were cut up; buttons were saved in a big tin and any usable material was saved to be used again later. I was still very young when I was taught to sew and I loved to rummage through the 'bit bag' to find pretty scraps of material to make oven gloves, needle cases, dolls' clothes or suchlike.

Grandma sometimes took me to visit her sister-in-law, Ada, and her niece, Elsie, who had a little china shop on Campbell Street. I liked our visits to see Aunt Ada – she

Me with my grandma.

seemed very old but she was very kind to me. Aunt Ada always enjoyed a chat, but I didn't mind how long I spent in the little shop because there were so many things to look at. I liked Aunt Elsie too. She used to tell me about all the different kinds of ornaments in the shop. When I was a bit older, she would tell me about her father, Tom, who was killed in action in the First World War. I could hear the sorrow in her voice; she was only five years old when her father died, but the loss was still very real to her more than fifty years later.

Whenever we visited Aunt Ada, we would walk up to look through the railings of Sep's churchyard at the sheep grazing among the headstones. I loved the sheep, and sometimes they would wander up and lick my fingers. My grandma was less impressed with them, as she thought it was disrespectful to allow them to wander among the gravestones, but I told her that if I were dead I would like to have the sheep there. Grandma would look across towards the church and when I asked what she was looking at, she would say that she was just remembering. I didn't understand at the

Elsie (*left*) and Lizzie Buswell outside their shop on Campbell Street, *c.* 1950.

Me in 1964.

time that so many of her memories were linked to that area. She grew up in Monks Pond Street but when she was in her teens, the family moved to No. 24 Campbell Street. Her sisters, Elsie and Lizzie, had their shop in Campbell Street. Grandma had worked with them, and when they died, the business passed to her. There must have been so many memories.

At that time, the redevelopment of the boroughs was underway, and it caused her great sadness to see the area reduced to rubble. In particular, she regretted the loss of St Andrew's church, where she was married. She conceded that many of the buildings needed knocking down but she said that she would have felt much better about it if they had replaced it with something better. She often said that they didn't know what they were doing by breaking up the communities, and she was convinced that they were stirring up trouble for the future. Perhaps she was right.

Grandma had lots of little sayings. If I whistled, she would inform me that, 'a whistling woman and a crowing hen is neither good for God nor men.' It didn't make much difference – I still whistled. She would often tell me to 'tell the truth and shame the Devil.' I wasn't so sure about shaming the Devil, but I soon learnt that it was a lot easier to tell the truth than to be caught in a lie. When she was feeling unappreciated she would say, 'You'll miss me when I'm gone,' and, of course, she was right – I missed her very much. She died suddenly following an operation just a couple of days before her eighty-third birthday. She had cancer of the cervix, which was entirely preventable and would never have happened if she wasn't such a prude. Unbelievably, she had suffered a prolapse as a result of giving birth and, rather than discuss such an intimate problem with a doctor, she had relied for nearly fifty years on the self-help measures available over the counter in those days! I think that perhaps she was ready to die. Life had moved on and she hadn't kept up, but I wasn't ready to lose her, aged just twelve. She was my link to the past and I still had so many questions to ask her.

Chapter Three

The Shop

My parents' newsagent's shop was on St James Road, just before the road divided to become Weedon Road and Harlestone Road, and many of my earliest memories are centred there. They had bought the shop in the mid-1950s and my father had big plans for his business. While I was still tiny, the shop was altered. A new glass frontage gave the shop a more modern look, the layout was changed and the shop was extended. The tiled floor, which was mostly light grey with an occasional red tile, provided a playground for me. I made up games, which involved hopping or jumping from one tile to the next, and of course I had to avoid stepping on the lines between the tiles because of some childish superstition. I was used to playing quietly by myself, and certainly didn't feel lonely or bored because there was always something going on and there was always someone to talk to.

The shop had a long counter. On the part nearest the till, there was room to display all the daily papers, then in the afternoon, the *Chronicle and Echo* (our local evening paper) would take their place. Back then, my parents still had delivery rounds, so the papers would be marked up for each route and put in large shoulder bags ready for the paper boys to deliver – they were mostly boys in those days. I rarely saw the morning paper boys because they had to complete their rounds before going to school and I wasn't usually in the shop at that time, but I got to know the evening paper boys. Sometimes the delivery driver was late and the paper boys had to wait around for the papers to arrive. Then, when the papers turned up, there was a frantic five minutes trying to get all the papers marked up for the rounds as well as dealing with the clamour of customers all wanting to be served at once because they had stood and waited for their paper. My favourite paper boy was a lad called Martin, who lived in Althorp Road. He was gentle and friendly with a lovely Irish accent. He must have been used to young children because he seemed to like talking to me and telling me stories about his siblings.

The rest of the counter was tilted at quite a steep angle with glass divisions to display sweets and chocolates. I could not see over the counter until I was older but there was plenty to interest me behind it. There was a section with cigarettes and cigars on display but I didn't pay much attention to them. It was a different world back then;

My parents' shop – my home until I was six.

smoking was accepted, but my parents did not smoke and they brought me up with the very clear message that smoking was 'not nice'. I have never smoked a cigarette in my life. The jars of sweets were much more interesting to me, and it seemed as if the shelving and the jars stretched all the way up to the ceiling. There were sweets of every kind and when a customer requested a quarter of sweets the jar would be taken down and the sweets would be tipped carefully into the shiny silver scoop on the big white scales. Then they were tipped from the scoop into a paper bag and the corners were twisted to seal the bag. My favourites were Callard & Bowsers blackcurrant and liquorice sweets. I loved the smooth hard outer shell, which tasted of blackcurrant, but best of all was the softer liquorice-flavoured filling. Sugared almonds were another favourite and I liked liquorice toffees too.

Beyond the counter there was a big display of magazines. I was too small to see the higher shelves, but the comics attracted my attention because they were at my eye level. Every week my father bought me a couple of comics; *Teddy Bear*, *Jack and Jill* and *Playhour* were among my favourites. I loved the pictures and the characters became familiar friends; my favourites were Harold Hare, Katie Country Mouse and Paddy Paws the Puppy. My grandma sometimes bought me a comic called *Sunny Stories*. It was the only comic that I actively disliked because it was a bit too 'worthy'. I thought it was boring, and it didn't interest me at all. I liked to read comics with my dad because he would tell me about the comics he read as a boy. There was a character called Tiger Tim in *Playhour* and my dad told me that the same character with his gang, The Bruin Boys, used to be in his comic. I think he said that the comic was called *Rainbow*, but I can't be sure. Comics sometimes contained a free gift. Usually it was something simple like a plastic glove puppet, a floppy plastic record or a sweet of some kind. When I was about five, my father bought me a new comic, which had bubblegum as a free gift. I was not allowed to have bubblegum, but he gave it to me anyway and taught me how to blow bubbles with it. When my mum and grandma got home, they were not impressed, but my dad just grinned at them.

As I grew up, I moved on to *Twinkle, Treasure* and *Beezer*. I also liked Beryl the Peril in *Topper* and Keyhole Kate in *Sparky*. Then a new comic called *Cor* came out – I was a fan from the very first issue. My favourite characters in *Cor* were Ivor Lott and Tony

Me playing on the 'roof garden' at the shop.

Broke. I was never very interested in *Bunty* and the like – I was too much of a tomboy to be interested in stories for girls. I read *Look-in* occasionally, but by then I had moved on to *Pony* magazine. I must have been about eleven when I discovered teenage magazines. My favourites were *Fab 208* and *Jackie*. Almost every girl I knew read *Jackie* from cover to cover and it remained essential reading until the end of my school days. I was a newsagent's daughter; newsprint rubbed off on me and I have never lost my passion for books and magazines.

The front of the counter below the newspapers and chocolate was a glass-fronted display cabinet with glass display shelves. Inside were rows and rows of Britains toys, cowboys, Native Americans (Red Indians as we called them in those days), wigwams, totem poles, soldiers of every imaginable kind, knights on horseback, knights in armour, farm animals, farm vehicles and machinery, horses, zoo animals, fencing, trees and gardens. It was just the right height for me to stand and look at all wonderful things and to hope that one day I would have my own Britains farm. My wish came true – I had a farm, a zoo and a garden, and they were among my best loved toys. Sometimes, when the shop was closed, my parents opened the display cabinet and allowed me to replenish the stock, as my little hands were small enough to reach in and line up all the different figures without knocking anything over.

There was a large display of cards along one wall, with coming-of-age keys, wedding horseshoes and boxed cards of every kind displayed on shelves above. Beyond the cards at the far end of the shop was my favourite area, the toy section. I was forbidden to touch, but I could look and I spent hours just looking at all the different things. High above me, tricycles, scooters and dolls' prams were displayed where eager little fingers could not reach them. The beautiful Wendy Boston bears gazed out from their display boxes and there were dolls large and small, dressed and undressed: baby dolls, teenage dolls, talking dolls, walking dolls and even dolls that wouldn't eat their greens! There were tea sets and printing sets, sewing cards and fuzzy felts. Matchbox cars, Corgi and Dinky toys, Airfix models and Action Man figures were there to tempt little boys of all ages – a few girls too! I liked toy cars, and had a number of Matchbox cars, as well as a selection of Corgi and Dinky vehicles, including a pink Lady Penelope Rolls Royce, Thunderbird 2 and a Batmobile. I didn't know many boys but I came to the conclusion that they were rather strange. I couldn't work out why they would waste hours building and painting Airfix models when they could buy ready-made boats, planes and cars from the Corgi and Dinky ranges, which were much nicer and didn't fall apart when you touched them!

There were all sorts of games from the tried and trusted Snakes and Ladders, flounders and tiddlywinks, to the new and extremely popular Mouse Trap. My parents ran a Christmas club, which enabled people to select the items that they wanted to buy and pay for them weekly over a number of months. The items were carefully wrapped in brown paper and put away on shelving near the stockroom.

We sold 'pocket money toys' too. There were lots to choose from, including card games, planes made from balsa wood, dolls' bottles with milk that disappeared when you tilted the bottle, little tea sets, puzzles of various kinds and many other things that I have forgotten. My favourite was a small box of rigid plastic body parts, called a Potato Man, but you had to find a real potato and fix the body parts to it to make the actual

Me 'helping' the electrician during alterations at the shop, 1965.

potato man. It was fun while it lasted but the rigid plastic parts broke too easily. I liked the colouring books and sticker books; in those days, we had to lick the back of the stickers in the same way that we used to lick stamps. The magic painting books were great fun too, and I liked the mystic pencil books, but the doll dressing books didn't interest me at all.

At that time, no one thought that toy guns were unsuitable for little boys, so cork guns, cap guns and guns in holsters competed for attention alongside bows and arrows and feathered headdresses. The brightly coloured feathers were very attractive to my young eyes and my toy cupboard already contained a rather splendid Red Indian headdress, a bow and arrow and a cork gun that made a rather satisfying popping noise when fired. Toys back then still reinforced gender stereotypes and my grandmother, who made disapproval a way of life, tried by fair means and foul to ensure that my toy cupboard contained only suitable 'ladylike' toys. She failed dismally because I was already a lost cause. I always preferred teddy bears to dolls, and I certainly didn't intend to miss out on toy cars and pop guns just because they were supposedly for boys. Soon after I was born, Grandma bought me a soft-bodied plastic doll with moulded hair. She wasn't the prettiest doll ever made, but I quite liked her when I was tiny. I called her Elizabeth. I enjoyed dressing and undressing her and I remember pushing her around in a little red doll's pram, but my strongest memory is of her blanket, which had a silky edge that I liked to hold when I went to sleep. Thankfully, my parents did not share my grandmother's old-fashioned ideas and I was given the freedom to be myself. My mother believed that a woman could do anything better than a man as long as she thought about it first. Her attitude made a big impression on me and over the years her example of strength and determination has given me the courage and confidence to tackle the many challenges of life.

There were many changes that affected the shop in the late 1960s and early 1970s. The first and possibly the most disruptive was the redevelopment of the area, which nearly killed the business because there were months and months of roadworks and people could not park outside. At times even pedestrians had to negotiate their way around roadworks to get to the shop. It seemed endless; the constant noise, dust and disruption was exhausting, but worse still was the rodent problem that seemed to be caused by the demolition of the buildings opposite. Everyone was troubled by mice, but our livelihood depended on making sure that they couldn't get at the stock, so a lot of money had to be spent on visits from a rodent control company and measures to protect the stock.

On 15 February 1971, we changed over from pounds, shillings and pence to the new decimal currency. A lot of planning had taken place and we had already seen some changes ahead of the move to decimal coinage. The new 5p and 10p coins had been in circulation since 1968 alongside the old shilling and two shilling coins. The new 50p piece had already replaced the old ten shilling note and the halfpenny and half crown coins had already gone, but still the change to decimal currency was viewed with trepidation by customers and shopkeepers. People carried little 'ready reckoner' booklets around with them and many, like my grandmother, complained with some justification that it was all a conspiracy to put prices up without people noticing. Grandma grudgingly adapted to the new decimal currency but she stubbornly refused to 'think in decimal', and for the rest of her life she converted everything back to 'old money' in her head.

On 1 January 1973, Britain joined the 'Common Market' (European Economic Community), and as a condition of our membership VAT replaced Purchase Tax in

April of the same year. From my parents' point of view, both were unwelcome changes and the introduction of VAT caused a lot of extra work, worry and expense for them. It was complex to administer and getting it wrong could leave a business facing a huge bill for back tax, so it was necessary to pay for professional help to complete the returns. It was a time of very high inflation, there was increasing unemployment, and strikes and industrial unrest were common. The National Union of Mineworkers was working to rule and as a result fuel supplies were dwindling, so the government introduced a three-day week to conserve fuel. Power cuts were common, but in the difficult economic climate shops could not afford to lose custom or let stock go to waste so they stayed open by candlelight. My father taped a wedge to the drawer of the cash register to prevent it being locked shut when the power went off. They just had to do the best they could and hope that things would improve, but it was a challenging time for the business.

Chapter Four

Time With Auntie

I can't remember a time when Auntie wasn't a very important part of my life. She wasn't really my aunt (she was a close family friend), but when I was still a baby, she offered to take care of me each week to enable my mum to spend time with her father, who was ill with cancer. So on Wednesdays and Saturdays, Auntie would come to collect me and take me to her house. I can still remember being pushed along in my pushchair over Westbridge past the station and on up the hill past all the shops in Gold Street, towards All Saints church. Then our journey took us past the Guildhall, past the United Counties bus station in Derngate and down Albion Place to her house.

When I was old enough to walk, instead of riding in my pushchair, my favourite part of the journey was the walk over Westbridge. I always wanted to see the trains and we knew just the right spot to get the best view; Auntie would hold me so that I could look over the wall at the platforms below. Sometimes the platforms were quiet and I would beg to be allowed to wait for the next train, but often there would be a train standing at one of the platforms. If I was lucky, I would hear a train in the distance and we would watch and listen as the sound intensified until the train came into view and slowed to stop at the station platform. Best of all was being able to see and hear a train as it was ready to depart – I liked the sound of the engine as the train pulled away and rattled over the tracks as it increased speed. I had a vivid imagination and I had several of Revd W. Awdrey's railway books, so it seemed quite normal to attribute a personality to the trains. If I had told my grandma that the trains had different voices she would have told me not to be so silly, but Auntie was different. She just smiled and said that perhaps they did. The part of the station that interested me most was the goods yard, but I couldn't see it from the pavement. I knew it was there because I could hear the railway noises at night and when I asked my dad what the trains were doing, he would tell me that they were shunting. Dismal, wet days gave me a chance to glimpse the goods yard because we caught the bus into town instead of walking, and Auntie would let me sit upstairs. If the traffic moved slowly, I could look over the wall for a fleeting moment before the trees and the tall advertising hoardings got in the way. I couldn't see much but I always hoped that I would manage to see more next time.

No. 13 Albion Place. (*Copyright J. Hendy estate*)

The other building on our journey to Albion Place that captured my interest was the Guildhall. I was too young and too small to appreciate the beauty of the building, and simply noticed the things that were low down at my eye level. I was fascinated by the low, narrow windows, which reached almost down to the pavement. They reminded me of the very narrow windows that you see on old castles, the sort designed for shooting arrows. I had a toy bow and arrow, but I think my limited knowledge on the subject of castle windows must have been gleaned from storybooks because, as far as I can remember, I had not visited a real castle. The low windows were protected by metal bars, and I felt sure that they must be dungeon windows. Auntie told me that there were some old cells somewhere under the Guildhall, but she reassured me that they were no longer used for prisoners, so I was quite safe. I believed her, but I made sure that I didn't get too close to those windows – just in case! The paving slabs outside the Guildhall were laid at an angle, so when we walked along the pavement they seemed to be diamond shaped, and Auntie told me that the paving was like that because the

The Guildhall, St Giles Square. This shows the 'diamond' pavement.

Guildhall is an important building. I don't know when the paving changed but the 'diamond paving' is long gone.

Auntie was always known to me as Auntie Buckingham. When I was learning to talk I was encouraged to call her Auntie Gladys, but I had trouble pronouncing her name, so forever afterwards, it was Auntie Buckingham and Uncle Bill. Uncle Bill's name caused me confusion too – it took me years to work out why his napkin ring had a W on it rather than a B! I grew to love them every bit as much as I loved my grandparents and spending time with Auntie was the highlight of my week. It was very different from the hustle and bustle of my home and I enjoyed the order and unhurried routine of daily life at No. 13 Albion Place. When we opened the sturdy, green-painted gate and stepped up from the pavement to the garden path, it felt as if I was entering a world where time behaved differently. The comfortable familiarity of my surroundings made me feel safe, and it was almost as if time stood still because nothing seemed to change. Looking back through adult eyes, I realise that keeping the house and garden looking clean, neat and unchanged must have involved a lot of hard work, but I wasn't aware of that at the time. As far as I was concerned, Auntie always had time to talk to me, to tell stories, play games and take me out for walks.

There were many lovely things in Auntie's house but my young eyes were not impressed by ornaments or beautiful furniture. I liked stories and the things that attracted my attention were items with a story attached. In the hall, almost opposite the door to the front room, was a large, shiny and very beautiful turtle shell leaning against the wall. I always stopped to admire it as I walked down the long hallway towards the back room, and I would ask Auntie to tell me about it. It had been caught by one of Uncle Bill's relatives and it had stood in the hall for as long as Auntie could remember. She had lived in that house all her married life and Uncle Bill had lived there with his father before that, so the turtle shell would have been very old. I was a very soft-hearted child, but I'm ashamed to say that at the time, I didn't spare a thought for the poor turtle. My head was full of stories and fairy tales and I didn't understand that a turtle was a real creature; I had never seen one, and I imagined that a creature with such a beautiful shell would be as magical as a unicorn. There was a shiny brass pan with a long wooden handle mounted on the wall in the hall, which Auntie told me was a warming pan. I was fascinated to know that, in the 'olden days' before hot water bottles and electric blankets, it was filled with embers and used to warm the bed.

In the hall at the foot of the stairs was an old and rather temperamental grandfather clock. The sound of the chimes was rich and pleasing and I liked to count as each chime echoed through the house. While Uncle Bill was still alive, the clock was reasonably well behaved, with just an occasional flight of fantasy where it would add an extra chime. Sometimes Uncle Bill would open the clock to show me the chains and weights inside and explain how it worked. He would remind me not to touch, but I was a well-behaved child and I knew that I must never touch because it was very delicate. I was fond of the clock, passing it each time I went up to the bathroom or into the front room. It seemed to me that it watched over all the comings and goings of the household from its position in the hall. As I grew up and Auntie got older, the clock became more eccentric – sometimes it would add an extra chime and occasionally it would lose an hour – but it still stood at the foot of the stairs and watched over the house.

I rarely went upstairs except to use the bathroom. The toilet was a little room close to the top of the stairs and the bathroom was next to it, above the dining room. It was a pleasant, reasonably large room with a lovely mixture of smells: soap, talcum powder and bath salts. There was a big old mirror on top of a white glass-topped bathroom cupboard and I liked to watch while Auntie tidied her hair and dabbed a dusting of powder onto her face. I rarely went into the bedrooms except to look in the toy cupboard with Auntie when we were choosing something to play with on a wet afternoon. There were four bedrooms, two on the first floor and another two on the floor above. An area of the house that I found far more interesting was the cellar. There was a door in the hall beneath the stairs which led down there, which I was absolutely forbidden to open on my own, because that was where Uncle Bill had his workshop. Sometimes, when he was working down there on a Saturday, I was allowed to go down and watch him as long as I promised not to touch his tools. There was so much

Auntie (Mrs Gladys Buckingham) at No. 13 Albion Place.

to look at that I was happy to stand quietly and watch him working. There were lots of jars and tins, which once contained baby food and now contained screws, nails and suchlike in assorted sizes. Uncle Bill was very patient – he would answer my questions and explain what he was doing. He seemed happy to encourage my interest in what my grandma would have considered 'boyish' things.

The front room was very big because it was really two rooms, with a bay window at each end. There was a piano in the back part of the front room as well as lovely ornaments and furniture. Sometimes I was allowed to 'play' the piano for a few minutes while we waited for the television to warm up for *Watch With Mother*. I can remember occasional visits from the piano tuner, who was blind. He spent a long time working on the piano and when he had finished he played some music to check that the sound was satisfactory. He played beautifully. The front part of the room was a lovely sitting room with an armchair and a sofa, which had a selection of comfortable cushions. There were usually cut flowers in a vase on a small table near the window and there was a television tucked away in the alcove between the fireplace and the window. The television had wooden doors on the front, a clear statement that it would not be allowed to dominate the room. Television did not take up much of my time at Albion

Place because there were many more interesting things to do. On Wednesdays, Auntie and I often watched *Watch with Mother* after lunch, while Uncle Bill had 'forty winks' in the brown fireside chair in the dining room before he walked back to work. The radio played a more important part in the daily routine of the house. Auntie listened to *Mrs Dale's Diary*, *The Archers* and *Woman's Hour* and, if we were at home at the right time, we listened to *Listen With Mother* together.

For the most part, daily life took place in the dining room at the back of the house. It was a nice room with a lovely big bay window, which looked out on an area of garden in front of the high wall of the house next door which, incidentally, belonged to an old lady called Mrs Rice at that time. In the summer, bright-coloured flowers cascaded from hanging baskets, but my strongest memories are of the beautiful laurel bush with big waxy leaves. I remember sitting at the table with my colouring books watching hesitant flakes of snow fall onto the laurel leaves and slowly slide off onto the ground below. I looked up at the sky and willed it to snow heavily enough for it to settle, but all it could manage were brief flurries, which faded away as soon as they reached the ground. Uncle Bill had looked out of the window at lunchtime and said that it would not settle, but I'd hoped against hope that he was wrong because I wanted to play in the snow.

A beautiful, polished table with matching high-backed chairs stood near the window – the colour of the wood always reminded me of the richness of a newly opened conker. When I sat at the table with my colouring books, Auntie would protect it with a thick pad, which fitted on top of the table with a heavy green tablecloth placed on top. At mealtimes, the heavy tablecloth was folded away to be replaced with an ordinary tablecloth. We set the table carefully with bead-edged cork mats for the plates to stand on and the cruet set in the middle, with the little silver salt bath next to it. I favoured my left hand and I struggled to get the knives and forks the right way round, but Auntie was patient and I was keen to learn. The items we needed to set the table were kept in a lovely sideboard, which stood against the wall opposite the window. There were glass decanters and attractive ornaments on the sideboard but the only things that interested me were the contents of the second drawer. It contained ink, pens, various writing materials, sealing wax and a beautiful, polished ruler, which belonged to Uncle Bill. It was not flat like normal rulers, instead shaped like a very narrow rolling pin. Sometimes I was allowed to use the ruler when I was sitting at the table doing some drawing or writing, but usually I just liked to hold it and look at the markings on it.

Uncle Bill worked in Castillian Street and he walked home for lunch, but I feel sure we called it dinner in those days. On warm days, I was sometimes allowed to stand in the front garden to wait for him. I liked the front garden. There was a tall hedge at the side of the garden path, so I had to walk all the way to the gate to look out for him. While I waited, I would walk around looking at the flowers and listening to the crunch of gravel beneath my feet. The garden was almost like a little knot garden; in the centre, there was a small tree encircled by a low hedge, and on either side of the circle, there were crescent-shaped low hedges with flowers planted inside. I was never especially interested in flowers but I liked the shapes made by the hedges, and the garden offered all sorts of possibilities for games of make-believe. There was a climbing plant growing to the side of the front door – I don't remember what it was called, but it looked nice in the summertime. The ornate, cream-painted, cast-iron decoration around the front porch fascinated me, and each time we came in or went out, my little fingers traced the curves and shapes of the ironwork. I grew to love that front door. It was solid yet beautiful – its highly polished wood was so smooth and shiny that it begged to be stroked. The brass letter box and doorknob were always shiny and there was beautiful stained glass in the top part of the door. The front of the house had a bay window on the ground floor with curved glass in the sides of the bay window. Below the window, there was an open area to allow light to reach the cellar window, but Uncle Bill had protected this with a translucent cover to prevent leaves and debris collecting in there.

We had our main meal at lunchtime when Uncle Bill got home. It was always a traditional meat and two vegetables-type hot meal. I liked meat and potatoes but I wasn't too keen on vegetables. Auntie understood this and only gave me a very small amount, but I was expected to eat what was on my plate. I had a deep hatred of Brussels sprouts and having to eat just two sprouts felt like an ordeal. My grandma would have made me sit at the table until I cleared my plate but Auntie was more understanding, and told me to put a little vinegar on them to improve the taste. It didn't make me a fan of Brussels sprouts, but it did make them somewhat less disgusting. After that, I used to eat my greens first to get it over and done with so that I could enjoy the rest of my meal. We always had afters and usually it was something with custard, but occasionally Auntie prepared my favourite, apple snow. Grandma never made it because according to her, it was not a 'proper pudding' but I loved it. I loved watching Auntie make custard, mixing a little milk with the custard powder, ensuring that there were no lumps, heating the milk in a saucepan and watching to catch it before it boiled over, then tipping it into the custard mixture, stirring briskly, and finally tipping it back into the saucepan to thicken for a moment or two. I think she must have made the custard before we ate our first course because once we had begun our meal, I would not have been allowed to get down from the table until it was over, but I have very clear memories of watching Auntie making custard.

I liked to stand in the kitchen watching Auntie as she prepared meals. The kitchen was fairly small and I had to be careful not to get in the way, so I would stand at the back and watch as Auntie cooked. There was an electric cooker against the wall adjoining the dining room, then a small work surface and corner shelving. The sink and draining board were below the window and then there were small corner shelves, with a free-standing wooden kitchen cabinet against the wall opposite the cooker. The kitchen was compact but very well organised. The cabinet had containers for flour, sugar and various other cooking ingredients, which fitted the cupboards perfectly. There was a white enamel work surface, which pulled out from the dresser for use when baking or preparing food. Sometimes I watched Auntie making cakes. Like my grandma, she checked each egg by breaking it into a cup before adding it to the mixture. She mixed everything by hand and was careful not to waste anything when she scraped the mixture into the cake tins. As far as I was concerned, she was a little too good at not letting anything go to waste, because scraping the empty bowl was the highlight of baking day. I expect it would be frowned upon these days because of the raw egg in the cake mixture, but I was given a spoon and allowed to scrape the last of the mixture from the mixing bowl and eat it – it was lovely.

Auntie was a very good cook, but she told me that when she first got married, she didn't know how to cook and they had to have someone to come in and help her until she felt confident. Perhaps that is why she was happy for me to watch and learn as she cooked. When I think of Auntie's kitchen, I remember the lovely smell of cooking that always made the kitchen feel welcoming. I was especially fond of a cloth bag containing string, which hung on the wall. Like my grandmother, Auntie saved string, brown paper and other materials that could be reused or put to another use. The bag had a picture of a cat and a kitten on the front with string threaded through a hole in the bag to look like the tail of the mother cat. The words, 'Don't pull my tail, pull mum's,' were written on the front of the bag. My strongest memory of the kitchen is the smell of Auntie's hand cream. A pot of Cremolia hand cream was kept on a little shelf near the sink and after doing the washing up, Auntie would open the jar and rub a little dab of hand cream onto her hands, putting a little dab on my hands too. They still make Cremolia and the smell of it brings back so many memories.

There was a back door leading from the kitchen to a porch area and a toilet to the left, before the steps down to the garden. I think the land at the front of Albion Place was higher than the land to the back of the houses. We went up a step from the pavement to the garden path and up another step from the path to the front door. Then, at the back of the house, we went down several steps to the back garden, so when I played in the back garden I was too low down to look through the kitchen window or the dining room window. It was a nice, neat garden with a lawn to play on, well managed flower beds to the side of the path and lovely hanging baskets on the side wall near the dining room window.

In the mornings, Auntie and I usually went out to do errands, and often we would walk through St Giles churchyard and on up York Road on our way to Cheney's butcher's shop. I think we used to buy bread from somewhere on Abington Square when we went to that part of town, but I don't remember exactly where. I remember our walks through the churchyard very clearly. It was so close to the hustle and bustle of the town but it was always calm and beautiful, with so many interesting things to see. Auntie told me that when my father and her son John were little boys, they went to St Giles School together. I liked to hear stories about my dad and I liked to look across at the school building on St Giles Terrace and imagine what it was like inside. Sometimes we would stop and look at gravestones and I would ask Auntie to read the names to me, but she was reluctant to do so and she would reassure me that the gravestones were very old. Perhaps she thought that I was too young to think about such things because it would worry me, but it didn't – I liked to know the names on the gravestones. I can remember that there was a lot of fuss because a decision was taken to remove some of the headstones and stand them against the walls of the churchyard. Auntie seemed quite sad about it. I remember discussing it with her one day. I was very young, but I told her that if all the gravestones were near the path next to the wall, more people could read the names and think of the people who were buried there. She smiled and said that I had 'an old head on young shoulders'.

Sometimes we would walk into town through the Co-op Arcade, which ran from St Giles Street across the little road called The Ridings and on up to Abington Street. I

St Giles church.

liked the way it echoed; it wasn't as echoey as The Emporium Arcade, but the tapping of women's high-heeled shoes as they hurried along still made a satisfying clatter on the tiled floor. The whole arcade was made up of different departments of the Co-op and we had to call into the grocery department to buy milk tokens. These were blue plastic discs that looked rather like children's play money and, according to Auntie, they were used to pay the milkman for the milk he delivered. When Auntie paid for the milk tokens she had to give them her Co-op number, which she recited in much the same way that people recited their phone number when answering the telephone. I remember asking my grandmother about milk tokens because our milkman was paid with ordinary money rather than milk tokens. She told me that our milkman didn't come from the Co-op and that no one would catch her messing around with milk tokens when it was just as easy to have the milkman from Northern Dairies and pay him in cash. When we came out of the Co-op arcade into Abington Street, we could see the Notre Dame Convent School a little further up on the other side of the road. When Auntie was a girl, she had attended that school, and sometimes she would tell

The market square on market day (Wednesday or Saturday).

me about being brought to school by a pony and trap from her home on a farm, in a village a few miles from the town.

We usually walked to the market to buy fruit or vegetables. Wednesdays and Saturdays were market days and the cobbled market square bustled with shoppers looking at the stalls. The market traders would call out the price of their products, but it was difficult to hear what they were saying because there were so many people shouting. Sometimes we would walk across the market square and through Osborne's Jetty to James Bros grocer's shop on the corner of The Drapery. My clearest memory of the shop is the smell. It wasn't a bad smell, it was a mixed up scent as if all of the fresh products were competing for attention. Occasionally, we would walk up the Drapery to Adnits department store, which I rather liked because I had been to visit Father Christmas there with my mum and it seemed magical. There were wide stairs down to the basement and up to the upper floors, but there was also a lift with an attendant to transport customers between floors. The lift was a bit of a novelty for me and I always hoped that Auntie would want to use it, but usually we had to use the stairs. On our way back to Albion Place, we would walk along Wood Hill towards St Giles Square, stop at the Corner House to buy a loaf then we would continue along St Giles Street to Lawrence's for me to choose a cake for my tea. I would spend a long time looking at all the cakes in the window but I usually chose my favourite, a vanilla slice. Auntie was

The Drapery looking towards George Row (*c.* 1950s).

very kind and understanding but, like the other adults in my life, she was very clear that I must eat properly and never 'mess around' with my food. The vanilla slice was a brave choice because the temptation to 'dissect' the layers was almost overwhelming, but at tea time, Auntie would cut it into slices so that it would be easier for me to eat without making a mess.

When we got back from doing the errands, we would have our elevenses, usually a milky coffee for Auntie and warm milk for me. It gave us a chance to sit and chat for a little while before Auntie began cooking. Often, I would ask her to tell me one of my favourite stories. I liked to hear about when Uncle John (her son) sat on a bee and got stung on his bottom when he was a little boy or about how her daughter had been such a poor little thing when she was born that they feared she may not survive and they had to give her something called Virol to make her stronger. Sometimes, Auntie would recite rhymes and poems to me, my favourite was, 'Two little kittens one stormy night, began to quarrel and then to fight ...'.

We often went out in the afternoons, weather permitting, but on wet afternoons we stayed at home and played games. I would go upstairs with Auntie to look in the toy cupboard, which once belonged to her children, and choose something to play with. My favourite was a Lotto game with the numbers stored in an ancient paper bag, which was so old and well used that it felt like soft cloth. I liked that game because

Auntie told me that my dad and Uncle John played with it when they were boys. Another favourite was the polished wooden solitaire board with the most beautiful marbles I had ever seen. I'm not sure that I knew how to play solitaire – I remember Uncle Bill sitting down to show me how to play, but I just liked to make patterns with the marbles. Other favourites included a box full of old dolls house furniture and the remains of an old and very beautiful doll's tea set. I would sit at the table and set out all the furniture while Auntie would tell me stories about the lovely doll's house that my grandfather Mick had made for her daughter, Betty. I was disappointed but fascinated when Auntie told me that the doll's house got woodworm in it and had to be burned. I wanted to see a woodworm, but Auntie said she certainly didn't want to see woodworm because she detested them even more than she detested bluebottles. She couldn't tolerate bluebottles – they would be hunted down, caught in a duster and dispatched. When Auntie explained that woodworm was a word to describe wood eating beetle grubs, I was less keen to meet one. I didn't mind beetles, but I didn't like the little grubs that sometimes got into vegetables, so I didn't think I would like beetle grubs very much.

Auntie would always sit down with me if we stayed at home in the afternoon. Often she would play with me or chat to me as she did some mending, but sometimes she would sit down with me and write a letter. Her daughter and son-in-law and their children had moved to Zambia for several years and Auntie missed them very much. Phone calls were difficult and very expensive so they depended on regular letters with precious, fleeting phone calls. Auntie would take her fountain pen, ink, airmail paper and the blotter pad from the drawer in the sideboard and settle down to write. She kept her writing small so that she could cram as much news and love as possible into the letter. Auntie had distinctive handwriting. It looked attractive on the page but was not easy to decipher, and cards and postcards from her had to be read several times in order to piece together the meaning.

She had four grandchildren. The older boy and girl lived near London and I saw them occasionally, when they visited. They were both older than me but I enjoyed spending time with them. The grandson and granddaughter in Zambia were closer to my age, one a little older and one slightly younger. I liked them too and I missed the granddaughter very much because we got on very well. I clearly remember when they came back to live in England permanently because Uncle Bill was so excited. I'm sure Auntie was excited too, but I think Uncle Bill's excitement sticks in my mind because normally he was a kind but very measured man, not given to displays of emotion. He borrowed my felt tips to make a welcome home banner. I was at school by then and was almost as excited as they were, especially when I was told that their granddaughter would be coming to my school for a little while. I looked forward to the day when she started school and I was so disappointed when they put her in a different class. I waited until break time, thinking that at least we would be able to play together, but when we got into the playground, everyone crowded around her and I didn't even get a chance to speak to her. I felt so sad that afternoon when I went home, having hardly had a chance to say hello to her, but things settled down and I enjoyed the time that she spent at my school.

Inside All Saints church.

Sometimes I went with Auntie to All Saints church, as she and a number of other people from the congregation took turns to help with the cleaning. She always introduced me to the people we met as 'our little friend'. I liked that because it made me feel very grown up. I was given a duster and was left to dust some pews while Auntie got on with her work. I dusted carefully and listened to the echoing sounds of voices and movements within the church. I looked around and thought about how different it was from St Andrew's Methodist church (the church that I attended with my family). All Saints had more sparkle and lots of decoration on the walls and the ceiling. Often, when I had finished my dusting, I would sit quietly waiting for Auntie and look around at all the patterns and pillars, wondering if God liked this church better than our rather plain one. I remember talking to Auntie about it one day as we walked home. Her reply was very simple but very wise. She said that she thought that God didn't mind so much about the church – he cared much more about the people in it.

Sometimes we went out in the afternoon to deliver the church magazine and I really enjoyed those outings because we visited places that I would not usually see. We would leave the house by the back door, walk down the grey brick garden path, past the large building at the end of the garden and out of the back gate. The building had big garage doors, which opened onto the little road at the back of Albion Place. I didn't think of it as a garage because it didn't contain a car. It contained much more interesting things such as deck chairs and garden items. In my memory, the building was of dark, almost black wood with white painted windows, but I think perhaps it may have been mostly brick with some wood. It was a nice, friendly building, which smelled of wood and creosote – it was far too nice to think of it as a boring old garage. Once outside, we walked down a little street into Swan Street and on through more little streets, delivering a magazine here and there on our way.

Our journey took us past a car park with some arches to one side, and some tall, old houses in the distance. I asked Auntie about the arches and I was fascinated when she told me that there had once been a railway station there. I wanted to know everything about it but Auntie wasn't very interested in trains. She told me that it had closed a long time ago, before the war. She also told me that the railway tracks had run over the top of the arches then over a road bridge and on past the edge of Becket's Park into the distance, all the way to Bedford. Auntie told me that the station building had once been very beautiful but after the station closed no one wanted to use the building. In the end, it looked very sad and unloved. She said that sometimes old buildings had to go to make way for new ones and the old station building had been demolished just before I was born. I really wanted to know more after that – I wanted to see pictures and hear stories about it, but it seemed to me that no one was interested in the old station. I was very surprised when Auntie told me that there had been another station in Bridge Street, and I was very excited when she said we could have a look one day. The station building was still there, though I think it had recently closed to passengers, but I was more interested in the level crossing and the signal box because you could get a very good view when a train came past.

We had to go under an archway to deliver one of the magazines to a house on Victoria Gardens and Auntie said she thought the people who lived there would have been glad

The signal
box and level
crossing, Bridge
Street.

when St John's station closed because it must have been very noisy living so close to the trains. She then added thoughtfully that it would have been hard for them to get their washing dry without it getting covered in soot and smoke from the trains. I didn't think I would have minded that too much if I could have watched the trains every day. We walked along Victoria Promenade opposite the cattle market. I had never been to the cattle market and I really wanted to know more about it. Perhaps wisely, Auntie told me that she didn't know much about it, but she said that she could remember when farmers walked their cattle and sheep to market rather than sending them in a lorry. I couldn't imagine that because Victoria Promenade was a very busy road and a lot of sheep or cattle walking to market would have caused chaos.

As we walked, we chatted about all sorts of things, walking past shops and through little streets, delivering a magazine here and there along the way. Sometimes there was a strong smell in the air, which Auntie said was the smell of malt and hops from the brewery. I didn't like the smell very much, but it was a lot better than the other smell that often wafted across the town centre. We were all troubled by the smell of the rendering plant in St Peter's Way and, depending on the wind direction, it often managed to drift all the way to St James, forcing us to keep our windows closed. Our journey took us across St Peter's Way to deliver a magazine to a house in Tanner Street. St Peter's Way had been built just before I was born and it seemed to slice through the area. It was very busy, and it was difficult to dodge between the traffic to cross the road. Tanner Street was close to a very large gasometer, which towered over the houses. Auntie said she felt sorry for the people who lived there because they had nice houses but they were overshadowed by the gasometer and they had to put up with the terrible smell from Bates rendering plant, which was close by. My clearest memory of St Peter's Way is of crawling along in rush-hour traffic on my way to school. When I was about five, I used to travel to school with my friend and her father, and it seemed as if the relatively short journey to Cliftonville took a very long time because the traffic moved so slowly. I didn't mind the traffic too much because I wasn't terribly keen to get to school and I liked looking out of the window at all of the buildings we passed.

I wish I had taken more notice of those walks through town delivering the church magazine because, over the coming years, almost everything on our route would fall victim to progress. The little streets and the last traces of St John's station are long gone. A supermarket now occupies the site of the old cattle market. The rendering plant is just a bad memory and now even the gasometers and Tanner Street are gone. The smells from the brewery still drift across the town centre from time to time, but the brewery itself is greatly changed. St Peter's Way remains, but it has changed considerably over the years.

Occasionally, in the afternoon, Auntie and I caught the No. 8 bus along the Billing Road to Park Avenue South, then we walked along the road that runs between the two parts of Abington Park to Abington church. Auntie made the journey to tend her parents' grave in the churchyard and I enjoyed accompanying her, because afterwards we would walk in the park and visit the aviaries to look at the birds. My favourite afternoon outing took us to Becket's Park, which Auntie always referred to as the Meadow. We would walk to the bottom of Albion Place past the ugly office block that looked so out of place next to the beautiful, old houses. Auntie told me that they had knocked down a nice, old house to build the office block. I think the ugliness of the new building grieved her far more than the loss of the old building. At the bottom of Albion Place, we went down the steep steps to Victoria Promenade and I held tightly to Auntie's hand as we dodged between the busy traffic to reach the park on the other side of the road.

Usually, we would walk down past the bowling green, towards the boathouse. I was afraid of water but I liked to watch from a safe distance when a barge came through

The bridge in Becket's Park.

the lock. Then we would walk alongside the river, staying on the park side of the safety rails and a safe distance from the water. Occasionally, there were barges moored along this stretch of water, but more often we would wave to a barge as it drifted past. When we came to the bridge, Auntie would stand and watch while I played. I had loved the humpbacked bridge since I was tiny. Auntie had taught me the nursery rhyme, 'The Grand Old Duke of York', and as I marched up to the middle of the bridge and then down the other side I chanted, '...when he was up he was up, and when he was down he was down...'. When I was tired of marching, Auntie and I walked over the bridge and a little way around the lake to my favourite spot – a small, concrete platform between the lake and the river, which allowed excess water from the lake to flow underneath and down what looked like little steps into the river. It was the ideal place to play 'pooh sticks', but we didn't drop litter into the water, just a leaf or a twig. The area around the river and the lakes was very beautiful, but if you looked beyond it, the skyline was dominated by ugly factory buildings and the tall cooling towers and chimneys of the power station.

We would walk back over the bridge and further on, following the river towards Bedford Road until we reached the playground, which was tucked away in a corner of the park. There were the usual swings, a slide and a seesaw, but my favourite was a long, bench-type swing, which my dad told me was called a 'jazzer'. A number of children could sit astride the bench seat, holding tightly to the handles, with legs dangling. It could be pushed by an adult so that the bench moved from side to side, or, better still, older children could stand at either end and control the momentum in much the same way that you could stand on an ordinary swing and work it by bending your knees and moving your body. I liked the idea that my dad and his friend John had played there when they were boys, and I loved to hear Auntie's stories about the things they did. I remember feeling absolutely devastated a few years later, when they took the 'jazzer' away because it was apparently unsafe. One of my other favourites disappeared from local playgrounds around the same time. It was known to me as a 'witch's hat' due to its shape, and had a bench seat around the base. The whole structure pivoted around a central pole, producing a fairly gentle but somewhat unpredictable ride.

By the time we got back to Albion Place, I was tired and ready for my tea. Usually, I had sandwiches of some kind – bread and honey was my favourite in those days. This would be followed by fruit, often a mashed or sliced banana, and then the cake that we had bought from Lawrence's earlier in the day. After tea, there was time to play for a little while before Auntie and I walked along to George Row to catch the No. 6, 6a or 12 bus to take me home. Auntie would bring the table lamp across to the table and I would sit quietly doing my colouring and looking at the twists in the lovely dark wood

My dad (*front*) and a friend playing in the playground.

of the lamp. Sometimes Auntie would ask if I wanted to take a sweet from the lovely old hinged tin that stood on the polished wooden trolley, close to the kitchen door. There were Foxes Mints, Nuttalls Mintoes, assorted toffees and Callard & Bowsers sweets. Occasionally, I chose a toffee, but usually I chose a blackcurrant and liquorice sweet. I would carefully unwrap it, pop it into my mouth and then Auntie would show me how to fold the wrapper to make a little boat. All too soon, it was time to get ready to go and catch the bus. I was happy enough to go home but I always looked forward to my next visit to Albion Place.

When the time came to start school, I was very upset that I would no longer be able to spend Wednesdays and Saturdays with Auntie and it took me a long time to settle at school. I need not have worried, as I still saw Auntie often. I went to Albion Place on Saturdays and sometimes Auntie came to meet me from school and I had tea at her house. I have so many good memories. Auntie was a constant in my life – always there, loving and unchanged when so many other things in my life were uncertain. I clearly remember when Uncle Bill died. I was in my first year at senior school and it came as a shock because I had not realised that his illness was so serious. It was less than three months after the death of my grandma and I felt very upset. These were the first significant deaths in my life because I had been too young to understand what was happening when my maternal grandfather died. I remember looking across at Auntie's house from the school grounds, longing to be able to comfort her, yet knowing that there was nothing I could do or say to make her feel better.

I missed Uncle Bill very much, but I still had Auntie and I saw her often. As I grew up, I knew that she was getting older and a little less vigorous, but her inner strength remained and for a long time she continued to live on her own and led a reasonably active life. When she died, twenty years after Uncle Bill's death, I was grown up with children of my own, but I felt the loss very deeply. It was hard to lose her, but I am so grateful for the special times we shared. She taught me so much about life, but two things in particular stick in my mind. When she made an arrangement she always added the phrase, 'all being well', because she knew that we could never take tomorrow for granted. She also set great store in wearing a vest, and whenever I had a cold or faced any sort of problem, she would mention that things would be better if only I would wear a vest. It made me smile then, and whenever I have a health problem, her words come to my mind and the memories still make smile.

Chapter Five

Primary School

School came as a shock to me. I didn't want to go because I was perfectly happy at home. I wasn't used to spending time with other children and my first weeks at school were frightening and upsetting. My parents had chosen to send me to Spring Hill in Cliftonville, which was the junior department of Northampton High School for Girls. It felt very big and frightening to me as an unhappy four year old, but it wasn't really. It was a beautiful house with a big gravel drive and a lovely garden. Cliftonville was a much quieter road than it is today, with allotments stretching back towards the Bedford Road on the land now occupied by Northampton General Hospital.

Several months before I started school, I went with my mother for an interview there. I don't remember all the detail of the interview, but I can remember a big front door and being taken away from my mother to talk to a teacher in another room. The teacher showed me a series of pictures and told me to tell her about the items in the picture. I was able to talk about all but one of the pictures. She seemed rather surprised and told me it was an orange, then she said that perhaps we did not have oranges at home. I was indignant – of course we had oranges! I explained that I knew what an orange was, but the picture looked more like a ball than an orange, and I went on to tell her about all the fruit in our fruit bowl at home. The 'interview' suited me very well because I was used to adults and reasonably confident when chatting one to one. However, when I got to school I was like a fish out of water because I wasn't used to children, and I felt completely bewildered. We had very small class sizes, but I felt lost in this crowd of people and I longed for the safety of home. My first term passed in a blur of confusion and misery, but when I returned to school after the long summer holiday, I had a different teacher called Mrs Mossman and at long last I felt safe enough to relax and enjoy some of the activities.

There were number cards and alphabet cards on the wall and every morning we recited the alphabet as the teacher pointed to each letter, then she pointed to the numbers and we chanted the numbers from one to ten. Our classroom looked out across the lawn, which was bordered by trees and shrubs, so we were very aware of the weather and the changing of the seasons. I grew fond of the smell of the classroom, which was a mixture of interesting things: plasticine, powder paint and polish, mixed

Spring Hill in Cliftonville, Northampton. (*Copyright Northampton High School*)

with the faint smells of lunch being cooked in the kitchen. The plasticine was kept in a large tin – it had been well used and the colours had all been mixed together creating a warm brown colour with a haphazard marbling of colour. I liked playing with plasticine. I would create long thin rolls and then I would carefully coil them together to create little pots. I liked painting too. I had always enjoyed drawing and I had paints at home as well, but the paints at school were better. I also liked writing – we were given paper and taught to copy letter patterns. I was quite good at copying lines and lines of 's' patterns, 'c' patterns and suchlike, but I used my left hand and the teacher kept taking the pencil and putting it in my right hand. I wish I had been brave enough to argue, but I wasn't confident enough to tell my teacher how hard it was to use my right hand, and gradually I got used to using my right hand as well as my left.

I wasn't too keen on learning to read. We had little red-checked gingham bags, which hung on the backs of our chairs to hold our reading books. We began with Happy Venture Readers, which I found deeply uninspiring. The books were about Dick and Dora, their friends, Jack and Jess, and their dog, Nip. It seemed to me that those books came out of the ark because the names of the characters were so old fashioned. As a child growing up in the 1960s, I didn't know anyone called Dick or Dora or Jack or Jess – I didn't identify with them and I couldn't care less about what the words meant because it was so boring. We had other books in the classroom that we could choose to look at and I found one or two of those more interesting. My favourite probably wouldn't be considered politically correct these days but I enjoyed the story. It was about a little boy who lived in the jungle and some tigers tried to steal his lovely colourful clothes; the story had a happy ending for the boy, but not for the tigers. We had better reading books later on – I think they were called Wide Range Readers – finally there was something worth reading! Suddenly, I could read, and by the time I left Spring Hill, I was in the top reading group.

In the summer we wore red, yellow or green gingham dresses, a blazer, a Panama hat and white gloves. I wasn't fond of the hat and I detested the gloves, but the dress and the blazer were reasonably easy to cope with. The winter uniform was very challenging for a young child, as it consisted of a navy blue pleated skirt, a navy cardigan, a white

Me in my school uniform on my first day of school, with the back of Althorpe Road and St James' School in the background.

shirt and a black and yellow school tie. This was worn with a gabardine raincoat, a hat and gloves, all in navy. By the time I started school, I could manage buttons, but the top button of my shirt was too stiff for my little fingers. I could produce something that (on a good day) resembled a bow to tie my shoelaces, but I just couldn't get the hang of tying a tie. I dreaded having to change for gym and dance lessons because it was such an ordeal. Thankfully, they changed the uniform after a year or two to a much more practical blue pinafore dress worn over a mustard-coloured turtleneck jumper with a Harris Tweed coat instead of the gabardine raincoat, so I was released from the worry of how to tie a tie until I moved up to Towerfield. The summer uniform also changed and our new summer dresses were made of a light blue or gold patterned material.

Our uniform had to be bought from Sanderson's on Kettering Road. I had never enjoyed shopping for clothes, but I hated shopping for school uniform. The uniform was expensive and it had to be bought with plenty of growing room, so it always involved trying on lots of different sizes and lengths, which I detested. We had to buy our shoes from Jones' in St Giles Street, which was another ordeal. We had to have indoor shoes, outdoor shoes, black gym shoes and dancing shoes. As I progressed through the school, the uniform requirements relaxed a little, but I vividly remember how much I hated my first pair of indoor shoes. They had an old-fashioned button rather than a buckle and aged four I couldn't manage the button on my own. Our school books were also bought from St Giles Street, from a shop called Savages, which was not far from Lawrence's. I rather liked going to that shop – I could have stayed there all day looking at the books.

I was terrified of Miss Beasley, the headmistress of Spring Hill, because she seemed to be very strict, but I only saw her at prayers in the morning so perhaps she was more human when you got to know her. I remember other teachers more fondly. Mrs Chamberlain, who taught me in Transition, was my favourite, but I liked most of the teachers. I grew fond of the buildings too. The rooms in the house were attractive with high ceilings and the staircase was beautiful, but I preferred the atmosphere of the annex. The hall, a cloakroom and two classrooms were in the annex, which you also had to walk through to the gym. I think it must have been a stable block in earlier days, but I liked it because it felt a little more relaxed than the main building. My First Form and Second Form classrooms were in the annex. I think Second Form was my favourite year at Spring Hill. It was the final year before moving up to Towerfield and I liked my teacher, Mrs Whysall, very much. Suddenly, it seemed that school was fun. Perhaps it was just because I felt more confident or perhaps it was because Miss Beasley had retired and we had a new and less formal headmistress.

Northampton High School was a girls' school, but a few boys attended Spring Hill until the age of seven; we had two boys in our class. In Kindergarten, we only went to school in the mornings and then, when we progressed to Upper Kindergarten, we stayed for two afternoons as well. From Transition onwards, we had one half-day each week. Most of us lived too far away to go home for lunch so we had to stay at school. Lunch was a very formal event with all sorts of rules to be observed; we had to have our own napkins and napkin rings and we had to say grace before we were allowed to sit down. We could ask for 'small' or 'ordinary' helpings but we were expected to eat all of the food on our plate. Second form pupils (aged eight) took turns as lunch monitors. They collected the plates from the staff who served the food and then they delivered the plates to the tables. The meals were quite nice, except on Fridays, when we had fish in parsley sauce with potatoes and mushy peas! I have always detested mushy peas, and fish in parsley sauce was not among my favourite meals when I was a child. I always asked for a small helping on a Friday but it was still a struggle to eat it because I hated the taste.

After lunch, we had a quiet time, which was known as 'rest'. We walked across to the annex and, after queuing to collect our rugs from the rack outside the cloakroom, we went to the hall, unrolled our rugs and lay down to rest. When we were all settled, stories were read to us by the teacher on duty: *The Borrowers, Milly Molly Mandy, Dr Doolittle, Sam Pig, The Country Child, 101 Dalmatians, The Moomins, My Naughty Little Sister, Paddington Bear, Little Grey Rabbit* and so many more good books. I loved them all and I can remember them very clearly so many years later. At the time, it just seemed like an enjoyable part of our daily routine, but I am sure that having stories read to us supported the formal process of learning to read by nurturing a less formal enjoyment of books.

Our school day was regulated by the shiny brass bell with a wooden handle that stood on the table outside the staff room. At the end of each lesson, a second form pupil would be given the responsibility of ringing the bell. First the bell was rung at the bottom of the staircase in the main building, and then it was carefully carried to the annex to be rung there too. Most of our lessons were in our form room with our own teacher, but we had specialist teachers for music, dance and gym. Music and dance lessons usually took place in the hall and we went to the gym for P.E. I was not fond of gym lessons, but they were preferable to dance lessons – I was not destined to be an athlete, and I was certainly not born to dance. Even my mother described me as a 'fairy elephant'. In a moment of total madness, my parents had paid for me to have extra dancing lessons, but even as a young child I had no sense of rhythm, no feeling for music and absolutely no desire to dance. To add insult to injury, I was required to wear a strange, pastel-coloured tunic and dancing shoes. I hated that tunic so much that I wanted to tear it to shreds! The dancing lessons made me so miserable that, after the first couple of terms, my parents allowed me to have elocution lessons instead and, much to my surprise, I enjoyed them very much. Music lessons with Mrs Willson, who seemed to be at least a hundred years old, were the worst part of my week. She stood us in a semi-circle and graded us according to our singing ability; I was always among the 'growlers' at the wrong end of the semicircle and I have disliked music ever since. She was right about my lack of musical ability, but to be written off as a failure at such a young age didn't help my confidence. Handwork lessons were much more to my liking. We did sewing, making such things as oven gloves and needle cases, weaving, raffia work, painting, making models with pipe cleaners, papier-mâché and junk modelling. I remember spending a whole afternoon making butter in a jam jar in Mrs Chamberlain's class. We each took turns to shake the sealed jar.

The nature table kept us busy all year round. In spring, we collected spring flowers, sticky buds and catkins. Then, as spring reached into summer, we saw tadpoles emerge from the frogspawn that we had collected. We watched, fascinated, as the tadpoles grew and gradually became frogs, and then it was time for them to be taken back to the pond or stream that the frogspawn had come from. We collected feathers, fragments of birds' eggs, scraps of sheep's wool, caterpillars, seashells, and even empty wasps' nests. The darker evenings and cooler days of autumn gave us an endless supply of fallen leaves in rich autumn colours. We made displays of leaves and we used them in our artwork. We collected acorns, conkers, berries of every kind and sycamore seeds, which fluttered down from the trees, spinning like tiny helicopters. As autumn gave way to winter, we collected pine cones, honesty and other dried seed heads, glossy holly leaves and bright red berries. In Transition, we kept silkworms in the classroom.

One of my fondest memories of Spring Hill is reading poetry in class every week. I enjoyed it very much, and became very fond of our poetry books, which were called *Rhyme and Rhythm*. I liked to read the poems again and again. The poems were fun – one of my favourites was called 'When Daddy Fell into The Pond' by Alfred Noyes, but best of all was the Spike Milligan poem, 'On the Ning Nang Nong'. As well as promoting a love of words and a desire to read, these early adventures provided a wonderful foundation upon which my lasting love of poetry was built.

The school day always began with prayers in the hall. As we filed into the hall, class by class, Mrs Mossman played 'Men of Harlech' on the piano. I don't remember much about prayers except that we always sang a hymn. My favourite at that time was, 'He Who Would Valiant Be', and my least favourite was, 'God Be in My Head'. I think we had a Bible reading and a prayer as well, but I really don't remember. At the end of each school day, we would line up in our classroom and our teacher would lead us across to the hall, where we sat cross legged in the care of the teacher on duty until our mothers came to collect us. Then, when our names were called, we had to walk across to the teacher, say, 'Good afternoon Mrs –' and hold out our hands to show that we were wearing our gloves (white for summer, navy for winter) and hats, before we were allowed to leave.

A couple of times each year, we put on our hats, coats and gloves and walked two by two along the Billing Road to 'main school' in Derngate. The 'toy service' took place shortly before Christmas; it was a whole school carol service and we all took gifts of toys to donate to charity. To me, it was an ordeal because main school was big and frightening and we had to spend weeks learning carols and practicing for the toy service. Sports day was even more of an ordeal. This took place towards the end of the summer term on in the main school grounds alongside Victoria Promenade. It was a very formal affair; our parents were seated in rows in the shade of the copper beech tree and the teachers were all in their best clothes. We had to practice the races for weeks before the big day. We even had to practice walking up to receive the winner's ribbon and shaking hands. For me, practice did not make perfect – I didn't win any races, so I was spared the worry of remembering how to shake hands properly. My greatest sporting achievement was coming second in the egg and spoon race!

I have lots of good memories of Spring Hill, but perhaps the most enduring memory is the smell of TCP and the row of pupils with cut knees, sitting in the First Form cloakroom waiting to have their knees bathed after falling over in the playground.

Spring Hill pupils ready to walk to the 'Toy Service' at Main School. (*Copyright Northampton High School*)

We took cut knees in our stride back then because we didn't have safety surfaces, but the staff must have looked forward to the summer when we were able to play on the lawn instead of the Tarmac playground and they could have a break from the constant stream of injuries.

At age nine, we left Spring Hill behind and moved to Towerfield in Derngate. The two years that I spent there were among the happiest of my school career. We referred to that part of the school as Towerfield, but it actually consisted of two connected buildings, No. 66 Derngate (Towerfield) and No. 68 Derngate. They were wonderful old houses with so much for inquisitive young girls to discover. There was a speaking tube and a dumb waiter between Miss Thornton's classroom on the ground floor of No. 68 Derngate and Mrs Nichol's room above. If you entered the building at street level, you had to go downstairs to reach the garden. There were cloakrooms downstairs in what were perhaps the old kitchens at No. 68 Derngate and there was a garden room below No. 66 Derngate. The gardens, which still retained some of their former charm, included a fish pond and a monkey puzzle tree. Beyond the paved area near the garden room, some steps led down to a long, narrow lawn where we played in summer.

The back of Towerfield and No. 68 Derngate in the 1980s. (*Copyright Northampton High School*)

There were still one or two private houses between Towerfield and main school, but a path bordered by an old brick wall led along the right-hand side of the Towerfield garden and around the back of the private gardens to the main school grounds. This enabled us to get to the main school without going out onto the street, but when we went to our music lessons at Becket House, on the corner of Victoria Promenade, we had to walk along the pavement to get there. Becket House was beautiful but it was rather creaky and it seemed unloved. It was our music department and we went there a couple of times each week for music lessons. Our music teacher, Mrs Turner, was nice, but despite her best efforts I hated music lessons and let my mind wander. I looked around at the interesting windows and the lovely ceilings with bunches of grapes in the coving and I tried to imagine what the house would have been like when it was a family home. I wish I had taken more notice of the wonderful buildings that were part of our school, but perhaps I was too young to appreciate them. No. 78 Derngate (the Charles Rennie Mackintosh house) was owned by the school at that time and the downstairs room was used as a classroom. I didn't have any lessons there, but I walked past it almost daily and I must have been into that classroom at some time or other, but I didn't give it a second thought.

We first met Mrs Nichol in Towerfield. She had a low, strong voice and a certain style and presence. She taught 'speech'. We had to write out and learn a poem every fortnight, and then, in the lesson, we took turns to stand up and recite our poem to her and the class while she marked the exercise book. Her marks were not generous, but just occasionally everything went well and she gave an A*. We soon learnt not to get into her bad books. She was firm but fair, and she knew how to get the best out of people. My parents wanted me to continue the elocution lessons, which were known as 'extra speech' lessons, and these lessons were taken by Mrs Nichol as well. We had to work hard, but I enjoyed working for Speech and Drama examinations. I perhaps didn't recognise it at the time, but Mrs Nichol played a significant part in my education

Me as a Towerfield pupil.

and I have a lot to thank her for. I am grateful that we were required to learn so much good poetry by heart. I have kept my *Poems for Pleasure* books from Towerfield days and they are among my most treasured possessions.

Mrs Noikavitch was my teacher for the first year at Towerfield. I liked her. Her room was upstairs in No. 66 Derngate. From the front window, we could look across the road towards the veterinary surgery of Sutton Steel and Holmes (where an office block now stands), and from the back window, we could look out over the gardens and the tennis courts, past the Cripps Block to Becket's Park and beyond. Most of our lessons were taught by Mrs Noikavitch, but music and games were taught by specialist teachers and Mrs Lett taught us history and biology. I enjoyed history and I was fascinated by biology, but Mrs Lett was a hard taskmaster. She made us copy notes from the board at top speed, and we had to write very fast because when she ran out of space the notes would be rubbed off and written over. Mrs Lett was a bit scary and I dreaded having to tell her that I had missed some of the notes because I couldn't write fast enough, but she was a very good teacher and she taught us well. The misery of swimming lessons began at Towerfield and my worst memory of my school life is being made to run from school to the Mounts for swimming lessons, it was all uphill and we had to run through the derelict streets near the Mounts that were awaiting demolition. When we got there, we had to change at lightning speed so that we had as much time as possible in the pool. I was always delayed by the struggle to get my very long and very thick hair into my swimming hat – it was agony to have that horrible hat stretched over my head. When it was time to get dressed again, the PE teacher did not allow enough time for us to get dry and dressed, so we ran back to school smelling of chlorine in a damp and bedraggled state. My long hair took hours to dry, so I spent the rest of the school day feeling damp and miserable. I was so pleased when, later in my school career, the pool at the hospital's Cripps Centre was used for swimming instead; at least we didn't have so far to run.

My second year at Towerfield was spent in Miss Thornton's class. I missed the warm, caring nature of Mrs Noikavitch, but Miss Thornton was interesting in a stiff and starchy sort of way. She sometimes took us out to explore forbidden parts of the garden and she told us about previous pupils that she had taught. I was amazed to find that Caroline Bradley (an international showjumper and one of my heroes at that time) had not only attended Northampton High, but had been taught in our classroom and had sat at one of our desks. Our desks were ancient, double desks made of heavy wood, with bench seats and desk lids that opened up so that we could keep our books inside. Each desk had an inkwell and a groove along the top for pens. When we moved from Springhill to Towerfield, we no longer wrote in pencil, and we had to have an Osmiroid fountain pen. At the start of each term, a brand new piece of pink blotting paper was issued to each pupil and we were expected to write neatly in our unlined exercise books, without blots. The inkwells were collected on a big wooden tray each week by the ink monitor and refilled with ink from a large bottle. We had monitors for everything: a door monitor to open and close the door when teachers or visitors came to the door (we had to stand whenever an adult entered the room), a book monitor to hand out and collect exercise books, a milk monitor to distribute our daily bottle of milk, and the most coveted job of all, a bell monitor who had to ring the handbell that stood on a table in the entrance hall at the end of each lesson.

At Spring Hill I was taken to and from school by car, but when I moved to Towerfield, I was expected to travel home by bus. On the days when I went to my parents' shop, I caught the No. 6, 6A or 12 bus from George Row to St James. On other days I caught the No. 8 bus (I think from Wood Hill, but I'm not sure) to Landcross Drive. Several of us caught that bus and then walked together along Abington Park Crescent to our homes. Unfortunately, there was not safety in numbers, and sometimes the girls from Abington Vale School would tease us or grab our hats and throw them into the road to get run over. We were too scared to remove our hats – it was a terrible 'sin' to be spotted by a teacher in uniform without a hat on – but having our hats damaged made our parents angry because they were expensive. Eventually, I found a solution to the problem; I avoided the girls by catching the No. 1 bus, which took me home via the Wellingborough Road instead.

Chapter Six

Growing Up

I was five when my parents told me that I was going to have a little brother or sister. I rather liked the idea, and I looked forward to having a sibling to look after. I had no idea how a baby was created – no one told me anything except that we would have to wait a few months and when the baby was ready my mum would go to the hospital to fetch him or her. I did not notice my mother's growing bump, and even when a school friend pointed it out to me, I insisted that she had not changed. I was also unaware of my grandma's extreme disapproval. Once again, she felt that her place within the family was threatened, and she was furious with my parents because she considered that they were being irresponsible. Two children six years apart is not excessive, but my grandma, who had never ever lived on her own, was afraid that there would no longer be room for her in our home. At first, my life continued much as before and I looked forward to welcoming a new brother or sister, but very soon the sense of security that I had taken for granted would be gone forever.

There was very little sadness in my life until I was six years old. The only occasion I can remember was when I was four. I'd had a little Jack Russell puppy for Christmas. She was mostly white with brown markings on her face and we called her Penny. I loved her very much and she was very attached to me but, as is sometimes the case with Jack Russell terriers, she was rather highly strung with a somewhat unpredictable temperament. My grandma was not fond of animals and they didn't seem to like her very much either; sometimes Penny would growl at her, perhaps sensing my grandmother's fear. My dad took responsibility for walking the dog and I usually went to Victoria Park with him. I liked to hold Penny's lead as we walked along Althorp Road towards the park and my dad would always tell me to 'wind it around your hand so she doesn't run away.' Penny was a few months old, with all the energy and exuberance of a puppy. She was only small, but she was surprisingly strong as she pulled excitedly on the lead on the way to the park. I don't remember all of the details of that last walk, but I was holding the lead (wound around my hand as usual) when Penny pulled and I tripped. Suddenly, I was being dragged along and my dad was shouting at me to let go of the lead, but I couldn't because the lead was wound around my hand. I could hear the fear and urgency in my dad's voice as he ran to hold on to me and suddenly the lead pulled

My new puppy,
Christmas 1965.

out of my hand and Penny made a dash for the park. I heard the noise of breaks and the squeals of pain and I saw Penny caught on the wheel of a van.

The next thing I remember is being back at home sitting on the storage heater (something that was usually forbidden) lost in sadness. I know that the van driver took her to the vet, but even as a four year old who believed in magic, I knew that there was no hope for Penny. In the distance I heard my dad say that it was his fault, but I knew it was my fault. I loved my grandma very much, but I still remember my fury when she offered me a drink and said, 'Never mind, it was probably all for the best.' My mum came home to find me still sitting on the heater, sad and silent, and her concern for me and her horror at what could have happened made her cross with my dad. I don't remember any more about that day, but I remember going with my dad a few weeks later to collect my new puppy. I had planned to call her Judy, but a puddle on the floor as soon as she got home led to her also being called Penny. She was a rough-haired Jack Russell with a pretty face and a much nicer temperament (but a deep dislike of milkmen and postmen). I loved her very much.

My dog Penny.

That had been the only cloud on my horizon until I was six. Then, on my dad's birthday in November, he woke with a headache and he felt unwell. It is difficult to put it into words but he wasn't quite right – he didn't seem to be making sense, and he just wasn't himself. My grandmother blamed the pomegranate that he had eaten on the previous evening, but the doctor diagnosed flu, and he prescribed rest. The headaches continued and the doctor variously blamed stress, overwork and exhaustion.

Christmas came and went, but my dad was still not back to his old self and my mum had to take responsibility for their business. In January, my brother was born and still my dad's health was causing concern. I would have preferred a sister, but I was happy enough with my baby brother. My parents asked me to help them to choose a name and I was determined that he should be called Willie after Willie Wombat (a character from a children's television show called *Tingha and Tucker*). My parents had other ideas and my brother was named Michael after his paternal grandfather. I was rather cross about the name, but I was the proud big sister and the next few weeks were taken up with new discoveries. I knew nothing about babies, but I soon found out about nappies, zinc and castor oil, bottles, gripe water and suchlike. I was rather partial to gripe water and I was always allowed to have a spoonful when my brother had some. Michael wore disposable nappies with a waterproof cover that clipped around them. My grandmothers both took turns to look after us because my father was still unwell and my mum had to run the shop and keep an eye on my dad.

My brother was a few weeks old when my mum told me that we were going to the cottage on Sunday afternoon to pick up the pram for my brother. I was excited because I loved the cottage and we didn't usually go there in the winter months. We all went; my grandma sat in the back with me and my brother, my mum was in the front and my dad drove. I don't remember much about the journey until we reached Kettering, then, unexpectedly, my dad pulled in to the side of the road. My mum asked if he

My brother with both grandmothers in 1968.

was alright, but he didn't reply – he turned slightly towards her and then slumped forward. I can remember my mum calling his name and screaming, my grandma went to a house and asked them to call an ambulance and I was taken into a house to wait with my grandma and brother. I don't remember how we got to Kettering Hospital, but I remember waiting in a room with my family and my aunt and uncle from the farm were there too. My dad was not dead, as I'd first thought, but he was seriously ill with perilously high blood pressure. I don't remember how long my dad was in hospital – I think it was about two weeks – but he was far from his old self when he returned home. The hospital doctor telephoned my dad's GP and he was furious when the GP still rambled on about my dad needing a holiday. My mum was told that my father needed complete rest away from the worries and demands of the business. Soon afterwards, my mum followed medical advice and arranged to take him to Devon for a break away from all the worries of everyday life.

Me on holiday in Devon with my baby brother and my dog, 1968.

We had our first holiday as a family at a beautiful house near Dartmouth, which was owned by my grandma's friend, Mrs Church. My parents had been there before and my dad had enjoyed many holidays there in his childhood, so it seemed like the ideal place for him to recuperate. It was March or April, so it wasn't exactly holiday weather and it was a very worrying time for my family, but I have some good memories of time spent with my dad while we were away. He told me many stories about the area; he shared his memories of childhood holidays there, but he also told me about being stationed in the area for a while during the war. He had to drive a lorry but it was hard to find his way around because the signposts had been taken down. He told me about a terrible tragedy that happened close by at Slapton Sands. It was one of the beaches used to practise for the D-Day landings in Normandy, but things went disastrously wrong and a lot of American troops were lost.

My father's heath did not improve, and it seemed as if the worries about his health overshadowed everything else. The details of what happened next are not clear in my mind; I just have fragments of memory, feeling invisible and terribly afraid. I had just broken up from school for the summer when my father was rushed to hospital. I wasn't at home when it happened. I remember my grown-up cousin, Carole, taking me to my grandmother's house in Kerr Street, and I remember that everyone was very worried. It seemed as if time had stopped. I don't remember being taken home and I don't remember anyone telling me what had happened. I just knew that my dad was very ill and my grandma told me that I had to pray for him to get better. Perhaps I wouldn't have understood if anyone had told me that he'd had a massive stroke, but not knowing anything was frightening.

My mum and my grandma were beside themselves with worry and exhaustion and I'm sure they had no idea that I overheard them talking about my dad. My mum had to decide whether my dad should have a serious operation. I didn't understand what a 'fifty-fifty chance' meant but, from what they said, it seemed to me that if he had the operation he could die and if he didn't have the operation he could die anyway. I was only six, but it seemed obvious to me that he had to have the operation because if he didn't, he had no chance of getting better. I know now that when my father got to hospital he was completely paralysed, but he had a little bit of movement in the toes on his right foot, which was apparently a hopeful sign. He was transferred to Oxford Hospital for more specialised treatment and my mum was told that he needed surgery to remove a blood clot from his brain. It was a very dangerous procedure but he survived the operation. He was in a coma for some time afterwards and he was in hospital for a very long time, or, at least, that is how I remember it. In the end, he discharged himself and got his mates from the Round Table to bring him home, but he was still very poorly when he left hospital. He had regained the feeling on his right side but he was still paralysed down his left side and he had to learn to walk again and to do all the things that we take for granted, such as getting dressed and using a knife and fork.

I loved my dad very much but his illness frightened me. In a way, it was easier for me when he was in hospital. I didn't need to worry about him as much because the nurses and doctors were looking after him, so to some extent I could relax when I was at home. That changed when he came home again, as I was frightened of his frailty

Me, aged five, sitting in a cardboard box with my dog. I loved playing with empty boxes.

and constantly worried about him. I found it hard to see him in so much pain and his frustration about being unable to do things for himself made me feel very sad. Very slowly, he taught himself to walk again and he gained some degree of independence, but he was in constant pain for the rest of his life.

My dad was not a good patient. He was very stubborn, he wouldn't accept help and he hated people fussing around him. My grandma didn't seem to understand that he was still an adult on the inside and, although sometimes he got muddled up and it would be a while before he could read and write again, he was still a man, not a child. She would see him struggling with his knife and fork and she would reach around and try to cut his food up for him, but my dad would slam his cutlery down and shout, 'If I can't bloody well cut it, I won't bloody well eat it.' I remember it vividly because swearing was something I hadn't come across before – no one swore in my family. My grandma would protest that she was only trying to help and then she would retreat to the kitchen with tears in her eyes. Perhaps the truth is that, even at forty-two, he was still her little boy; she had been so afraid of losing him when he was in the Army and now all those fears had come flooding back. My dad had been provided with a tripod walking stick to help him to learn to walk again, but he wouldn't use it. He waited until he was on his own and then he dragged himself out of bed by hanging on to the furniture; sometimes he fell, but eventually he learnt to stand. Then, when he could stand, he gradually taught himself to walk by leaning against the wall and hanging on to the furniture. Eventually, he could walk without a stick, which was so much more than anyone dared to hope for, but it was not enough for him. He knew that he was a shadow of his former self.

I remember it as a very dark and frightening time for all of us, but it wasn't all bad. One of our customers, a lovely lady called Daphne, offered to help by taking our dog to the park and if I was at home, I was allowed to go too. I had always liked Daphne and going for walks in Victoria Park with her enabled me to hang on to a little bit of normality; it was nice to talk and laugh and do ordinary things for a little while. I spent Saturdays and occasional afternoons after school with Auntie Buckingham, in Albion Place. I loved spending time there, I felt safe and comfortable and I could relax and be myself.

As my dad gradually got better, I felt more comfortable spending time with him and I have some happy memories of things that we would never have had time to share if he had been well. Sometimes he told me stories about his childhood – he seemed to remember the past better than the present and I enjoyed his stories. He often told me about the old electric trams. He was born towards the end of 1925, so he could remember when Northampton still had trams (I believe they continued to run until about 1934). He also told me about the introduction of traffic lights, which I think was at the very end of the 1920s. Apparently, the lights were activated by a car driving over a strip on the road, but my dad and his friend found out that they could make the lights change by jumping up and down on the strip. Their antics led to them being told off by a policeman and, no doubt, he got a telling-off from my grandma as well. I remember him telling me about when he was a telegram boy, his first job after leaving school. He taught me to recite the names of the poet streets in Kingsley in the correct order and he told me that he knew every street in the town. The best part of his job was taking telegrams to the New Theatre in Abington Street, because it enabled him to meet some of the people who performed there and he was able to build an interesting collection of autographs. I still have his autograph book.

We couldn't do some of the things that we used to do. I missed walking in the park with him and I missed all the ordinary little things like sitting down on the stairs to drink a milky coffee after the shop closed on a Sunday morning. One thing that hadn't changed was my dad's sense of fun and his determination to be himself. He used to tell me stories about when he was a little boy and about the things he and his dad used to do together. My grandfather had died long before I was born but I got to know him through my father's memories. He was a quiet, gentle father, who clearly loved his son very much. He let my dad do things which my grandmother would never have allowed, such as bringing his rabbit into the house on a Sunday evening while my grandma was at church. At the time, I just enjoyed the stories, but now I can see that my grandfather loved my dad for who he was. He allowed him to have fun and he didn't feel the need to push him or change him. My grandmother loved him very much too, but she couldn't help pushing and nagging. I don't know if my dad ever thought about it in that way, but throughout all the uncertainty of his illness, one thing was never in question – I knew that he loved me. He didn't push me to achieve and he didn't try to change me, he just enjoyed being a parent and sharing some fun of his own childhood. He taught me how to listen to the football scores being read and to tell by the pitch of the announcer's voice if the home team had won, drawn or lost, which was great fun. My grandma was horrified when he taught me how to blow bubbles with bubblegum, but my dad just grinned. When he taught me to whistle, she said, 'A whistling woman and a crowing hen is neither good for God nor men.' Her disapproval just made me whistle all the more!

Chapter Seven

A New Home

My parents had been planning to move away from the shop before my father became ill. They had looked at a number of houses, but they hadn't found anything that suited them. After my father's illness, it seemed even more important to have a home away from the business so that my father could have a little more freedom. My parents had friends, who lived in Ridge Way, Weston Favell, who told them about a house for sale in a quiet cul-de-sac just around the corner. In some ways, it was perfect because it was quiet, there were good schools nearby and Abington Park was a short walk away, but I don't think my parents had anticipated some of the difficulties that they would encounter. I don't remember much about the move to Hillside Way, but I remember my mum showing me my new bedroom. They had bought a new bedroom set for my room, a matching wardrobe, chest of drawers, dressing table and stool; it was modern and very nice, but it is difficult to get excited a about a wardrobe when you are seven. I was much more concerned that my floor-to-ceiling toy cupboard was too small! There was also a new ottoman for my room, white with a pattern of pink rosebuds on it – I have never been a pink rosebud sort of person and I didn't like it very much.

I hadn't been keen on the idea of moving, I was very happy in my old home and I didn't want to leave it. The thing that troubled me most was that the sounds were different in Weston Favell. When I went to bed in my old room, I listened to the sounds of the station and the goods yard; I liked the noises and I liked to think about the trains as I went to sleep. My new home was strangely quiet, except for the mournful calls of wood pigeons, and I longed to hear 'my' trains so much. It was much quieter in the daytime, too; I missed all the traffic noises, the chatter of people in the street and the excited voices of the children in the school playground. On Sunday, we heard the church bells from St Peters church, which were more tuneful than the Boys Brigade band, who used to parade past the shop on the way to church. Nevertheless, I preferred the band.

There was new furniture downstairs too: a long, modern sideboard, a lovely extending dining table with matching chairs and a big wooden radiogram to replace my dad's old record player. There was a new table in the kitchen as well. It had a blue patterned Formica top with four wooden stools with matching blue seats. After all the trauma and exhaustion of the previous year, my parents needed the move to be as

Our new home
at No. 11
Hillside Way.

easy as possible, so the house was redecorated before we moved in and all the carpets, curtains and furniture came from Phillips in Abington Street. My father knew the two sons through the Round Table and they dealt with everything from measuring up to fitting the carpets, hanging the curtains and installing the furniture. The only large items to come from our old home were our beds, the three-piece suite and the old, faithful Hoover Keymatic washing machine. Phillips was a lovely shop but it closed down two or three years later when the town centre was redeveloped. Their premises were at the end of a row of shops, which were demolished in about 1972 to make way for the Grosvenor Shopping Centre to be built.

Our new house was nice. It had an open-plan lounge and dining room, with big windows and a French door which leading to the back garden. There was a cloakroom and a toilet downstairs as well as a good-sized kitchen with a built in larder. Upstairs, there were four bedrooms, a bathroom and an airing cupboard. It was lovely to have a garden at last; the lawn was large enough for us to play but small enough to be manageable. A gate in the back fence opened onto the allotments, which seemed huge. They stretched almost as far as Church Way and St Peter's church and they seemed to fill all the space between Ridgeway and Bridgewater Drive. I was not allowed out of the back gate, so I had to be content with the garden. There was a flower bed, which sloped down from the lawn towards the house, with steps down to a small area of crazy paving next to the house. I was fascinated by the large, concrete coal bunker – I had never seen one before. A path led around the house from the drive at the front, through the side gate, past the kitchen door to the coal bunker at the back of the house. So, when the coal was delivered, they just carried it to the coal bunker in big sacks, lifted the lid and tipped it in.

The house had central heating but there was a fireplace in the lounge and we often had a coal fire in the winter. My grandma said that it made it feel more homely. I liked to help my grandma to make the fire in the morning. The tools used for the fire hung on a little stand on the hearth: there was a poker, a brush, tongs and a small shovel. It was called a companion set. We would use the poker to rake the ashes through to the bottom of the fire and then we would use the tongs to pick up any partly burned lumps of coal and set them aside on some newspaper. After that, we could pull the heavy metal front piece out of the way, remove the grate, sweep everything into the sunken ash container and then carefully lift it out and carry it out to the ash box. We always referred to the dustbin as an ash box. It was made of heavy, galvanised metal with a metal lid, and the ash from the fire was put in it along with all the household rubbish. When we had replaced all the parts of the fireplace, we began to build the new fire with coal from the coal scuttle, which stood at the side of the fireplace, using kindling, a firelighter and knots of specially folded sheets of newspaper, which grandma taught me how to make.

The telephone and telephone directory sat on top of a low, built-in cupboard in the alcove between the front window and the fireplace. A cable connected the phone to the wall and the handset was connected to the base with a coiled cable, which had a tendency to tangle. If you wanted to make a phone call, you had to sit in the chair next to the cupboard. The phone was cream, with a clear circular plastic dial on the front with ten small finger holes around the edge of the dial. A number was printed at the side of each hole; the last number was zero, not ten. There was something very satisfying about dialling a number, but you had to be careful because it was easy to misdial. You had to select the correct number, put your finger in the hole and guide the dial around until your finger reached the metal 'stopper', and then you had to remove your finger to allow the dial to return to the correct position before dialling the next number. I knew all our family phone numbers by heart, but we had a telephone book with the names and addresses of all our friends written in it. We had what was known as a party line, which was shared with the house next door, and every so often, when we lifted the receiver to make a call, we could hear them talking on the line and sometimes when we were using the phone, we could hear them attempting to dial a number. It was very inconvenient, but I think we had to have a party line because of limited capacity at the exchange or something of that sort.

The cupboard under the phone was packed with tinned food of every kind, including fruit, vegetables, ham and salmon in considerable quantities. Grandma said that if visitors turned up unexpectedly she would always be able to provide them with a meal, but I think her need to store food probably had more to do with her memories of times when food was scarce. Her parents had a lot of mouths to feed so she was often hungry as a child, and as an adult she had coped with food scarcity and rationing during both

My dad with Hillside Way in the background.

wars. Providing enough to sustain her family must have been a constant worry during those long years of rationing, so it is hardly surprising that she felt the need to have well stocked cupboards.

When we lived in St James, there were a number of shops close by, but there were fewer shops within walking distance of our new home. Sometimes we walked with my grandmother to the small supermarket in Park Way – I think it may have been called Civils, but I am not certain. It sold all the basic groceries that we needed but it was very small, so sometimes we walked to the Spar shop in Landcross Drive instead. We could only buy as much as we could carry comfortably because we had a long and weary walk home. A mobile greengrocer came to Hillside Way once a week, so my grandmother bought most of our fruit and vegetables from the mobile shop. She was very fussy and had to look at everything before she bought it, and she would tell the man in no uncertain terms if he had poor quality produce. I looked forward to the arrival of the mobile shop because my grandma always bought me a Wagon Wheel chocolate-covered soft biscuit. I'm sure Wagon Wheels were much bigger in those days!

Moving to a cul-de-sac meant that, for the first time in my life, I had a certain amount of freedom. There were other children living in the street and my parents allowed me to go outside to play with them. I made friends with a girl called Susan, who was a year younger than me; she lived next door so we played together often. Susan introduced me to her other friends and before long, I felt at home. Most of the children in the street knew each other from school but I went to a different school so I missed out on some of their shared experiences. My parents were perhaps wise not to move me to the local school. I had taken a long time to settle at school and I'd had to cope with a lot of anxiety and disruption in my home life, so it was probably best to avoid further change.

I enjoyed spending time with Susan's family. Her mum didn't go out to work and she often found interesting things for us to do. Mostly, we played outside and amused ourselves, riding our bikes, taking turns to play with Susan's stilts or my pogo stick or bouncing around on our space hoppers. We enjoyed playing on our roller skates – they were the old-fashioned type that fit over our shoes, so that when our feet grew, we

The No. 1 bus turning round at the Trumpet (the terminus at that time). In the background is the post office in Park Way where I bought sweets.

adjusted the skates to fit our new shoes. Hillside Way was built on a hill, as the name suggests, so as you went down the road, each house was a little lower than the previous one. Our house was semi-detached so that it was joined to Susan's house. Her house had a flat driveway but our drive sloped steeply to the road, making it perfect for roller skating. Despite the stern warnings from our parents, we would start at the top by the garage door and skate down the drive and straight into the road. There were a few cut knees, but we were used to that; we didn't have safety surfaces in those days and no one paid much attention to minor cuts and bruises. We played in the back garden too. I had a lovely big swing that my uncle had made for me and a trampoline that my parents had bought for my birthday. All my friends liked to play on the trampoline and when we were tired out from jumping we could throw a blanket over the trampoline and turn it into a den, lounge on it and read comics or just look up and watch the clouds float across the sky. My little brother loved to dig so my parents had a wooden sandpit made for him and he played there for hours with his Tonka toys: he had a dump truck, a crane, a cement mixer and an excavator. Considering the amount of redevelopment going on in the town, it is hardly surprising that my brother was obsessed with diggers and building sites.

The street was still being built; it seemed as if they completed one house before starting the next, so there was always a building site somewhere down the street. The area was not fenced off as it would be these days and, despite the warnings from our parents, it was very tempting to children. Poppies grew in the disturbed ground and the newly dug foundations were good hiding places. As the walls grew out of the foundation trenches, the temptation to walk along them was irresistible. One day, I lost my balance and fell off one of the low walls and hurt myself quite badly on the metal parts, which protruded from the wall within the foundation trench. I got a severe telling-off from my grandmother and another from my mum, but it was my dad who ensured that I would stay away from the building site in future. He explained to me that building sites contain many potential dangers, but more importantly he helped me to understand that, without meaning to, we could easily damage the work that the builders had already done and it would cost time and money to correct.

Susan and I did lots of things together. She would come to my house to play or I would go to hers. She had a dressing-up box with an interesting selection of garments, which allowed our imaginations to run wild. I had piles of comics, which we would sprawl on the floor and read on rainy days and we both had an assortment of toys, but more often than not we chose to play outside. We both had bikes and, after much persuading, our parents allowed us to ride them to the post office in Park Way to buy a few sweets. Fruit Salad or Black Jacks were the best value, but I liked liquorice bootlaces best of all. It was on these trips that Susan taught me the childish superstitions that the children passed from one to another on their way to school. The very attractive thatched house on the bend, leading from Weston Way to Ridge Way, was known to us as 'the Witches' Cottage' and, to stay safe, it was necessary to hurry past quickly. There was a house towards the top of Ridgeway that had a number of gnomes in the garden. According to childish rumour, the woman who lived there didn't like children and it was safer to avoid the house by crossing over to the other side of the road. It was also necessary (for reasons long forgotten) to avoid stepping on the cracks between the paving stones, so, to us, the short and very safe walk or bicycle ride to the post office was an adventure fraught with dangers.

I often went to tea with Susan, and sometimes she would come to tea at my house. I liked her house because it wasn't open plan like ours. I liked her family too and they were very kind to me. It seemed to me that her family life was a little more structured than mine, which is probably due to our different family circumstances. Susan and her sister had to do chores, just little things like setting the table, helping with the washing up or dusting, but she could not come out to play until her chores were done. I was also asked to help with little jobs around the house, but it was more informal, being expected to help when asked rather than having daily chores. Susan and her sister went to bed a little earlier than I did, and before they got ready for bed, their mum would read them a chapter from their bedtime reading book. Sometimes, I was invited to stay for the bedtime story and I was introduced to some wonderful books. Most of all, I remember the stories of Mary and Laura from the Laura Ingalls Wilder books.

The bottom part of Hillside Way had not been built at that time. There was rough ground that sloped down towards Abington Park Crescent and Bridgewater Drive, with a well trodden path that people used to cut through to Abington Park Crescent. My grandma sometimes took us that way when we went to the park or to the Spar shop on Landcross Drive. On our side of Hillside Way, there were only two houses after our house (we lived at No. 11), and beyond the houses was some rough ground with a little spinney, which bordered the allotments. It was a good place to play because it had lots of potential for scavenger hunts, making dens and suchlike, but the land was needed for building and before long, the trees were felled and the little spinney was nothing more than a fond memory. Susan became a fond memory too, when her family moved to Cheshire. We kept in touch, but I missed her terribly.

There was not a Methodist church nearby so my dad decided that we would go to the local church instead. Our home was actually in Abington parish, but St Peter's, in Weston Favell village, was closer, so that is where we went. I went to Sunday school in the morning and then I went to Evensong with my dad and my grandma. I didn't mind Sunday school – the teachers were nice – but I didn't like going to Evensong very much. It seemed to go on forever and all that chanting seemed very strange to my young ears. I can still remember most of it and I can appreciate the beauty of the words now, but I couldn't then. I used to wonder if God got bored too. I contented myself with counting the number of pages left and checking the time. On a good day, we could get home in time to watch most of *The Brothers*. I went to Brownies at St Peter's too. I wasn't unhappy there, as the lady who ran it was very nice, but I became increasingly reluctant to go and when the time came to move up to Guides, I decided to leave. By then I had other pastimes. I had been taking riding lessons and my interests were focused around horses. My parents bought me a pony called Geme for my eleventh birthday. We kept him at Brampton Stables and most of my free time was spent at the stables riding him and doing all the other jobs associated with owning a pony. When I was at home, I read books and magazines about ponies and I watched television programmes about horses, including *White Horses*, a dubbed version of a German series, *Follyfoot* and

A recent postcard of St Peter's church.

Black Beauty. I also loved to watch *The Royal International Horse Show* and the *Horse of The Year Show* – my parents gave me special permission to stay up late to see it.

Abington Park was only a short walk away. I was never allowed to go there alone, but I was taken there often. Grandma took us to play in the park and, usually, our walks took us around the big lake. We fed the ducks and the swans, and I liked to find a quiet spot to stare into the water looking for fish – there were some big fish in the lake. In the summer we would take our fishing nets and a little bucket to fish for tiddlers. We caught a crayfish once but we put it back because it seemed rather fierce, and on another occasion we caught a newt. It was interesting to look at but, after we had admired it, we put it back in the lake. We used to put the fish back too, because they wouldn't survive for long in a small bucket of water. I was always being warned to be careful and not to get too close to the edge. I didn't fall in, but my little brother did once. Poor grandma had to cope with a drenched and tearful three year old and a rather smug big sister – she scolded both of us all the way home!

The aviaries, which were tucked away at the side of the museum, were always my favourite part of the park. I would stop to look at each cage in turn, trying to identify

THE LAKE, ABINGTON PARK, NORTHAMPTON

Abington Park lake.

all the birds without reading the labels. The last cage was the peacock enclosure and I would stand there for ages watching them and hoping that one of the peacocks would display its tail feathers for me. I have fond memories of the playground too: the tall metal slides that were too hot to touch on sweltering summer days; the metal 'spiderweb' roundabout that seemed to go so fast that it made your legs feel wobbly when you got off; the seesaw, which was much more fun than it looked and, best of all, the big swings, which could go so high that you believed that you might go right over the top. We didn't think of the playground as unsafe; we had fun, and the occasional bumps and bruises taught us to be careful.

In the spring, we watched the ducklings and cygnets as they swam with their parents, but we were careful not to get too close because the swans were very protective of their young. During the summer, my mother would sometimes take us to the park after school. We would sit on the grass at the side of the play area and have a little picnic, and then she would watch us while we played. When it was time to go home, we would stop to buy an ice lolly from the Gallones ice cream van, which always parked opposite the church in Park Avenue South, within sight of the play area. As summer faded away, we searched under the horse chestnut trees for conkers and we watched as the squirrels scurried around collecting acorns. Then, as the year drew onwards, we waded through carpets of fallen leaves admiring the colours and textures of autumn. Winter brought its own beauty, with frost on the bare branches and ice on the lakes, which we were strictly forbidden to walk on. Best of all was snow, which turned the park into a magical world filled with excited children on sledges. I had a beautiful wooden sledge with blue tubular metal runners.

Winter brought a lot of problems for the residents of Hillside Way. It was a cul-de-sac and it didn't get much traffic so, when it snowed, the road was not gritted. The snow compacted and the road became so slippery that it was impossible to get cars up the hill and round the tight turn at the top of the road. This was a big problem for my parents because their shop had to open every day, regardless of the weather, and they had to get there one way or another. My dad had special winter tyres for his car, but there were still times when my mum had to walk all the way to shop because they just couldn't get the car out. It was much too far for my dad to walk, so my mum had to cope without him. I realise now that life must have been very hard for my mum; she had a lot to cope with and a lot of responsibility. We all had to cope in our different ways; my dad had to deal with his disability, he was in constant pain and just doing ordinary things required extraordinary effort. I had to cope with fears that I didn't really understand, a fear of illness and a constant dread that my dad would collapse again when there was no one around to help. In the early years after his stroke, he blacked out often and sometimes he hurt himself badly when he fell. It made me very scared and constantly worried about him. Eventually, he was seen by a doctor who understood what was causing him to collapse and he was prescribed a new medication, which helped a lot. My overwhelming memory of our years in Hillside Way is of waiting – it seemed as if I spent my life waiting for my parents to get home. The shop took up so much of their time and effort. It provided a living for them but it demanded so much that they had very little time to enjoy life.

Chapter Eight

Kerr Street

My mother grew up in Kerr Street, an ordinary terraced street in the centre of Northampton. It ran down from the Upper Mounts towards Wood Street, which in turn led into Abington Street. If you looked up Kerr Street, you could see the fire station on the opposite side of The Mounts. Like most of those old terraced streets, Kerr Street contained business premises as well as residential properties. My grandparents, Emily and Charlie Griffiths, lived at No. 19 which, if you entered Kerr Street from The Mounts, was on the right-hand side a little more than halfway down the road. I remember there was a shop next door, which sold ballet shoes and clothing for dancers, called The Stage Door. Beyond that was a depot for the Walls Whippy Ice Cream Company and ice cream vans were often parked in the street. Further down towards Wood Street there were other business premises, including Soutar Thorne, which was a leather company.

By the time I knew Kerr Street, it had already started to change, the shadow of demolition hung over the town centre and in a few short years Kerr Street and all the surrounding streets would be gone completely. My mum remembers the street very differently, for as long as she can remember, the buildings that became the ice cream depot were occupied by Burbidges, a funeral company, which also provided wedding cars and taxis. She remembers hearing them still working in the building at the back of the premises late in the evening after she had gone to bed. The shop next door to my grandparents' house, which I remember as The Stage Door, had once been an old bakehouse with a flat above the shop and the main bakehouse building at the back. My grandmother spoke of people taking their Sunday dinner to be cooked at the bakehouse, but by the 1930s, when my mum was a child, the business had moved to Regent Square. After that, the building was empty for a while before being used to accommodate evacuees during the war, then for some time afterwards it was used as living accommodation. It was empty for quite a long period before the little shop opened in 1960s.

My grandparents' home was a three-storey property with a small garden at the back. When you walked through the front door there was a long narrow hallway that was always referred to as 'the passage'. The passage was very dark, with no windows and

Me at the back of my grandparents' house in Kerr Street.

brownish wallpaper; it led to the back room, which in turn connected to the kitchen. As you walked down the passage, there was a door to the left, which led to the front room, and then, a bit further on, the stairs ran up to the left before you reached the living room door. The stairs were steep. There were two bedrooms on the first floor, one at the front and one at the back, and more stairs led up to the other two bedrooms on the top floor. My mother shared the back bedroom on the top floor with her sister, Betty, and their older sister, Joan, had the front bedroom. My grandparents slept in the front bedroom on the first floor and my great-grandmother had the back bedroom. During the war, the family had to take evacuees, so for a while my aunt had to give up her bedroom and all three sisters had to share the back room. My mum wasn't too keen on that because she had to sleep in the middle.

The front room was kept for best, and was always neat and clean with lots of interesting ornaments. It had a small, old-fashioned, black fireplace, but the fire was never lit so it was cold and not as welcoming as the back room, which was the heart of the house. I often asked to go into the front room because I liked to look at the ornaments, but I was always closely supervised by my grandmother. Sometimes I would look out of the window at the other houses and I would ask my grandmother to tell me who lived in each house. It seemed as if she knew everyone.

The back room was warmer and more homely. It had three doors: the one that led to the passage, one that led to the kitchen and a door that led down to the cellar. In earlier years, the cellar had been a very important part of the house, but by the 1960s it wasn't used very much. When I was little, the living room had a tiled fireplace and hearth, but that was a relatively recent alteration; when my mum and her sisters were children, there was a black range fireplace in the living room. It had a fire in the middle with an oven on the left and a very small oven on the other side. By the 1930s, when my mum and her sisters were growing up, the oven was not used for cooking very often because there was a cooker in the kitchen. The kettle was boiled over the range fire, there was a grille over the fire for the kettle to rest on and my aunt remembers that her grandmother would keep her teapot on the hearth. When the range was eventually taken out, my grandmother was delighted with her new tiled fireplace because it was so much easier to keep clean. The old range had to be black leaded every Friday, a very dirty and time-consuming job.

Emily Griffiths with two of her grandchildren, sitting outside the back door of No. 19 Kerr Street around 1950.

The kitchen was long and narrow and it always felt cold. There was a step down as you entered the kitchen from the living room and on the left there was a door that opened on to the back yard. The house did not have a bathroom or an inside toilet. You had to go out of the back door and down the path to get to the outside toilet, which was built next to the end wall of the kitchen. The lack of a bathroom did not seem to bother my grandmother greatly; in fact, she often pointed out that it was an advantage having their toilet close to the house because a lot of people had to walk to the end of the garden to reach their toilet. However, there were some practical difficulties; my mum remembers having to ask someone to go down the garden with her if she needed to use the toilet during the evening because it was very dark, especially during the wartime blackout. When I was little, the toilet had a cistern high on the wall with a long chain, which you had to pull to flush it, but my mum can remember when they didn't have a flush toilet at all. When she was young, the toilet was more like a wooden bench with a hole rather than the sort of seat we're used to now. It had had the necessary pipework to take away the waste, but when they went to the lavatory, they had to take a bucket of water with them to flush it after use. Getting a flush toilet was seen as a great luxury.

There was a grey metal bath hanging on the wall outside the kitchen. When my mum and her sisters were children, they had a bath in front of the fire every Friday night. My grandmother would put the clothes horse around them to keep them warm and shield them from view. The clothes horse was always in use. Washing was dried outside whenever possible, but it had to be aired before being put away. In those days, it was quite normal to only take a bath once a week, but the family were never dirty. They had what my grandmother referred to as a 'strip wash', standing by the kitchen sink with a bowl of hot water. When they reached their teens, the girls were allowed to go to the 'new baths' on the Mounts for a slipper bath once a week, which cost sixpence each. My mum recalls that the men's baths and the women's baths were completely separate. You had to queue up and wait your turn, and then the assistant would run the bath for you and show you to your cubicle. You had to take your own soap, towels and whatever you needed, so it was still quite an effort to have a bath. Before the Mounts Baths opened in 1936, it would have been necessary to walk all the way to the Corporation Slipper Baths on the corner of St Andrews Road and Spencer Bridge Road, which had opened in 1928. I think before that it was a choice of the tin bath or no bath at all.

The metal bath was used on washday too. When my mum was little, my grandmother had a big mangle outside, and when the clothes had been washed and rinsed, my grandmother set up the mangle with bath below to catch the water as she turned the big, heavy handle to force the washing through the mangle. It was a difficult job because at the same time as turning the handle she had to reach around to prevent the clean washing dragging on the floor as it emerged from the mangle. Eventually, the copper was replaced by a Burco wash boiler and the heavy old mangle was replaced by an Acme wringer, which clamped onto the sink. Washday was still a bit of an ordeal and the metal bath was still needed to catch the water that spilled over the sink, and then to carry the clothes out to the washing line, but at least my grandmother didn't

My grandmother Emily standing at
the back door of No. 19 Kerr Street in
the late 1950s.

have to stand out in the cold to use the mangle. Eventually she had another boiler with
a wringer on top, but I don't think she ever had an automatic washing machine.

My grandmother liked nothing better than a nice cup of tea, so she would often pop
into the kitchen to put the kettle on. She had a whistling kettle, which she heated on the
gas cooker. It made such a noise as it boiled that it was impossible to ignore; she found
the whistle reassuring because it meant there was no possibility of leaving the kettle to
boil dry. I liked to sit on the living room step to watch my grandmother while she was
busy in the kitchen and occasionally, as a treat, she would put a little bit of butter on a
teaspoon, dip it in the sugar bowl and give it to me to eat. I can only remember small
details about the kitchen. There were coloured rubber ends on the taps which made it
easier to direct the flow of water. There was no fridge; instead, eggs, butter and other
items were kept in a meat safe, which was a free-standing cupboard with fine metal
mesh on the front and the side to protect the food from flies and to provide good
ventilation. I found it fascinating – if I stood close to the mesh I could look through
and work out what was inside.

My mum has clearer memories of the kitchen. When she was a child, my grandmother
had a built-in copper boiler in the far corner of the kitchen against the wall, which
connected with the house next door. On the end wall of the kitchen in the opposite
corner to the copper, there was a brick arch, which looked as if it had been part of
a fireplace, and there had once been a sort of hearth there too (it was where the old
black stove had stood). The house had mains water, but my mum can remember that

there was a water pump, which stood behind the kitchen door near to the sink. It had been boxed in with dark wooden casing, leaving the arm of the pump sticking out. The pump did not work, but when she was younger my mum liked to pump the arm up and down. Eventually, the arm was removed because it got in the way.

I don't remember my grandfather, Charlie, very well; I was only three when he died. I remember sitting at the table watching him build playing cards into a tower and hoping that he could use all the cards before the tower fell down. I can remember his lovely smile – when he laughed his whole face seemed to crease up. Most of all, I can remember his long pants; when I was playing on the floor, I would look up his trouser leg and his long pants came all the way down to his socks. He was a fishmonger and he had to stand in the cold while he prepared the fish, so he wore warm underclothing.

After a brief spell in a shoe factory as a boy, he began his working life as a butcher. He worked for Stowe's, which was on the corner of Whitworth Road and Billington Street and, like many butcher's shops in those days, there was a small slaughterhouse attached to the premises. It is hard to imagine how someone as gentle and kind-hearted as my grandfather coped, but he learnt his trade and remained with the company until 1930 when he was twenty-nine years old. He left because he was offered the chance to work for F & W Hunt at their shop on the Wellingborough Road, almost opposite the turning to Victoria Road. The fishmonger's shop sold game as well as fish, which was apparently common practice in those days. My mum remembers that their neighbours relied on my grandfather for little favours, such as humanely killing poultry with one quick movement of the neck. Sometimes, a neighbour would come to the door with a

Charlie and Emily Griffiths with one of their grandchildren in the back garden of No. 19 Kerr Street in the 1950s.

hare, a rabbit or a game bird of some description, asking if Charlie could please 'see to it' for them. They would hand it to my mum or one of her sisters and they had to take it in and hang it on the hook at the top of the cellar steps. My mum remembers it clearly because she liked to stand and watch her dad as he skinned the rabbits or plucked and prepared the birds. She didn't like it when there was a carcass hanging on the hook at the top of the cellar steps because she would have to look at it every time she went down to the cellar. Coal was kept in the front cellar (it was dropped through the front cellar window when it was delivered), and in the back cellar milk was kept cool on a slab and meat and other perishables were stored in the meat safe, so there would be many journeys up and down the cellar steps every day.

I have to rely on my mum's memory and the stories that she has told over the years because I never went down into the cellar. All I can remember is the heavy curtain intended to stop draughts, which covered the cellar door in the living room, and the grating just outside the back door which I was scared to step on. I believe it was there to let the light into the back part of the cellar. My grandfather was a very practical man. He had a workbench set up in the back cellar; it was very cold, but he often worked down there. He had a last next to his workbench, which he would use to repair shoes; like most people in Northampton, he had links with the shoe industry. His father and other family members worked in the shoe trade and his first job after leaving school at the age of about twelve was in a shoe factory in Talbot Road. My aunt recalls that my grandfather was very good at woodwork and he made some of their furniture, as well as a lovely doll's house and other toys for the children. If anything needed mending, it would be taken down to the cellar for him to work on.

My grandmother was a tiny woman, both in both height and build, but she had a quiet strength and determination. She wasn't formidable like my other grandmother, but she set a lot of importance in keeping up standards and doing what was right. Before she was married, she worked at the Brook clothing factory in Clarke Road; she was good at sewing and knitting and she made nice clothes for her children. My aunt recalls that her best dress, which was only ever worn on a Sunday, would be shop bought, but everything else was handmade by my grandmother or cut down and altered from clothes that were passed down by friends. My mum was the youngest of three sisters, so clothes, including 'Sunday best', were passed down to her from her older siblings, but my grandmother always made sure that the girls were clean, neat and well turned out.

My cousins, who are a little older than me, remember the ritual of scrubbing the doorstep; it seemed to them that my grandmother and her neighbours had a competition to see who had the cleanest step. My grandparents' doorstep was not very high – it was hardly a step at all – but further up the street towards The Mounts, some of the houses had steep steps. My aunt remembers that the neighbours used to chat to each other as they scrubbed their doorsteps, and they used to scrub a small part of the pavement in front of the doorstep as well. My grandmother was rather reluctant to embrace change. This was partly because of her beliefs, but mostly because she was afraid of electricity. She would not buy anything on a weekly payment scheme or suchlike; she believed that it was better to save up and wait until she had enough money to buy whatever was needed. My aunt remembers that for years my grandmother flatly refused to have a vacuum cleaner in case it caught fire. They didn't have fitted carpets, just Lino and rugs, or 'mats', as my grandmother called them. She would sweep the mats with a brush and then from time to time she would take them into the garden, hang them over the washing line and beat them with a stick to get the dust out. I remember her using a carpet sweeper, but I have no recollection of her using a vacuum cleaner. As well as her deep distrust of electricity, my grandmother was afraid of fire and thunder, but more than everything else she had an irrational fear of mice, so the family always kept a cat in order to keep mice away.

All of the grandchildren have happy memories of time spent with our grandparents in Kerr Street. My cousins remember that when the fire station siren sounded, my grandmother would run up the street with them so that they could watch the firemen slide down the poles and drive off in their fire engine. I don't remember the poles, but I remember watching the fire engines drive off with their sirens sounding. I also remember when our fire engines were painted yellow instead of the usual red, but thankfully it wasn't too long before we had red fire engines again. My cousins remember that my grandfather would sometimes give them a toffee from the cupboard at the side of the fireplace next to his chair where he kept his toffees and walnut whirls. I liked it when my grandmother told me stories about her three girls: one used to get into trouble for admiring herself in the mirror when she was at the table, one used to hide her crusts under her plate because she didn't like eating crusts and my mum got told off for not sitting properly on her chair. My mum and her sister, Betty, sometimes got in to trouble for tying their bed sheets to the bedposts to make a tent. Apparently, my mum was a bit of a tomboy when she was little. When she finished telling me about her three girls, she would tell me that one day she would have three little boys and call them Shadrach, Meshach, and Abednego. I didn't know that she was teasing me or that she was past childbearing age, but I knew the Bible story of how God saved them from the fiery furnace.

My grandfather, Charles Griffiths, at the back door of No. 19 Kerr Street in the late 1950s.

My grandmother knew the whole of Robert Browning's very long poem, 'The Pied Piper of Hamelin'. I don't know when or why she memorised it, but it probably had something to do with her chapel. I liked it when she recited the poem, but other family members groaned when I asked to hear it again. My grandparents attended Artizan Road chapel, and when it closed, the family went to Princess Street Baptist chapel. My grandmother was a good singer and could play the piano; when she was younger she often sang at various chapel functions and suchlike. I remember her singing hymns occasionally, as she knew the words to all of the hymns when *Songs of Praise* came on the television and she liked to sing along. More than anything, I remember her singing a song to us about 'Darling Mabel'. I think she used to sing it to help my little brother get to sleep. I had a toy piano and I can remember my grandmother teaching me to pick out tunes, such as 'Nelly Bligh Caught a Fly' and 'God Save the Queen' with one finger. She played the piano well, but by then she had passed her piano on to her oldest granddaughter; I am not sure how she developed her love of music, but I know how she learned to play the piano. When she was a young girl, there was a piano shop called Judges on the Wellingborough Road and when their daughter was a baby, my grandmother used to take her out in her pram and look after her, and in return she was given piano lessons. She worked at a clothing factory prior to her marriage and she made up her mind to save up for a piano. She chose the piano that she wanted and she paid money to the shop out of her wages every week until the piano was paid for and she could take it home.

I remember going with my grandmother to Mr Dick's shop just around the corner in Lady's Lane. It was only a small shop, but it seemed to sell everything. My cousins remember that he used to make lollipops in a mould, which you could buy for a penny, but I don't remember that. Occasionally, my grandmother needed to 'run an errand' and we would take a short walk into town, down Kerr Street, across Lady's Lane, down Wood Street and into Abington Street. At that time, there were still a number of butchers, grocers and food shops in the town centre, and my grandmother used to buy her meat from Wallington's, which was on the corner of Wellington Street. She shopped for food every day or two as she needed it, so she didn't have heavy bags to carry and she didn't have to worry about keeping things fresh. There was no need for my grandparents to own a car; everything they wanted was within walking distance and there was a good bus service if they needed it.

I think it was around 1969 when my grandmother left Kerr Street. It changed considerably during her last couple of years there, was due to be demolished and gradually her neighbours were moved out to other accommodation. Many of the residents had lived there for a very long time, I don't know exactly when my great-grandparents first moved to Kerr Street – it was sometime after 1911. I know that my grandmother lived at No. 19 with her parents prior to her marriage, she was married from there and my grandparents began their married life in the flat above No. 17 Kerr Street. They moved into rooms in Norman Road, Abington, when their second child was expected, but by the time my mother was born three years later in 1930, the family had moved back to No. 19 Kerr Street because my grandmother's father had died and my great-grandmother needed help. Kerr Street was a community; the people who lived there looked out for each other and understood one another because over the years

Abington Street, Northampton.

they had shared each other's joys and sorrows. I wonder if anyone understood at the time that when they demolished those streets that they destroyed far more than bricks and mortar – they devastated a community. The neighbours were scattered across the town and all the roots and landmarks of their lives were lost; shops, pubs, churches, chapels, schools and social clubs were all reduced to a heap of rubble.

My grandmother moved to a lovely little flat at the bottom of Norman Road, within easy walking distance of our home in Weston Favell and my aunt's home in Birchfield Road (by then my other aunt had moved to Essex). It was a lovely flat, with a small balcony that looked down at the large communal garden below, and just beyond there were cattle grazing in the field. She could look across the Wellingborough Road to Abington Park Crescent and watch the comings and goings of the traffic. The flat was comfortable; it had a nice bathroom and a much more practical kitchen. It seemed ideal for her, and the neighbours were friendly, but it wasn't the same as the sense of community that existed in Kerr Street. From my point of view, it was lovely to have my grandmother living close by. I enjoyed spending time with her and I especially enjoyed going shopping on Birchfield Road with her because we always popped in to see my aunt and uncle at their newsagent's shop. Sadly, my grandmother didn't thrive in her lovely new flat; she could no longer just pop into town or run round the corner to the shop, her chapel was gone, the shops that she had used for years were gone. She didn't complain, but she seemed lonely despite daily contact with her family. I don't think any of us really understood that the move left her feeling isolated and took away her freedom and independence.

My final memories of Kerr Street are very sad. As the occupants of the houses were moved out, some of the properties were boarded up, others were let on short term tenancies and some were occupied by squatters. It no longer felt the same, no one seemed to care about the houses and the street felt unloved and a bit frightening. My grandmother began to feel anxious and unsafe in her own home and by the time a council property became available for her, she was ready to leave the home that she had lived in for most of her life. The redevelopment of the town was often referred to as slum clearance. Kerr Street wasn't a slum- the houses needed to be modernised, but they were no worse than many of the terraced houses on the opposite side of The Mounts, which survived. When I was ten or eleven, we used to run from our school in Derngate through the town centre to our swimming lessons at the Mounts Baths. The route took us up Kerr Street, and by then, the houses were boarded up and the street looked very sorry for itself. My friends didn't like it because they were afraid of rats, but I found it terribly sad because I could remember how it used to be.

Chapter Nine

Leisure Time

My parents' business gave them little freedom. The shop had to open every day to sell newspapers so they had to make the most of the limited free time available to them. During the 1960s, Northampton still had a half-closing day, so on a Thursday afternoon the shop closed at lunchtime and reopened to sell the evening newspapers at 4 p.m. It only gave them a couple of hours to themselves, but at least they could enjoy an unhurried meal together on a Thursday. The shop opened just as early on Sunday mornings as it as it did on other mornings, which was about 5 a.m., and it was surprisingly busy. Early in the morning, coachloads of men heading out for a day of fishing crowded into the shop to stock up on sweets, cigarettes, newspapers and magazines. Then, as the morning progressed, people who lived nearby called in for their Sunday papers, pop and treats. By the time the shop closed, it was almost lunchtime and my parents had already done the equivalent of a full day's work. We would sit on the stairs and enjoy a milky coffee together before restocking the shelves with sweets and cigarettes ready for the following morning, and only then could they turn their back on the shop and escape for the afternoon.

During the first six years of my life, I can only remember us going away together for more than a just a Sunday afternoon outing once. We went to see Aunt Chris in Wales, who lived in a village called Ffrith not far from Wrexham. She was my grandma's sister-in-law, my grandfather's older sister and the only one of his siblings that I can remember. Aunt Chris seemed very old, with lots of wrinkles, but she was less stiff and starchy than my grandma. I liked her and she made a big fuss of me because I had been given her name. My parents had not set out to name me after her – it was a coincidence – but Aunt Chris took it as a great compliment. I don't have clear memories of the visit because I was very young, but I can remember sitting on her doorstep and going for a little walk with her. I don't know how long it took us to get there or how long we stayed, but at most it was probably only overnight. Perhaps we even managed the whole trip in a day but, if so, it would have been a very long day. As far as I know, that is the only time that we were able to go away as a family. Any other time off had to be taken individually and during my first six years, my parents didn't even take holidays together.

In Wales visiting Aunt Chris (*right*), my grandma (*left*) and my Dad holding me, June 1963.

My mum, dad and grandma each had a different half-day off every week, so when I was little I had an opportunity to spend time with both parents individually. It didn't make up for the lack of family time, but I have some very happy memories of outings and activities with each parent. My dad enjoyed driving so we often went out in the car together – sometimes he would take me to Thornby to visit a friend of his, who was known to me as Uncle Frank. I enjoyed those visits very much; Uncle Frank had a big white goose, which he said was better than any guard dog. The goose came to the gate as soon as we arrived, it hissed and flapped at my dad and it wouldn't let him in until Uncle Frank came out, but it was always nice to me. Perhaps it was because I was too young to show fear or perhaps it didn't see me as a threat, but it would let me go through the gate without any fuss at all. Uncle Frank was old and he lived alone with his dog. He seemed to enjoy our visits and he liked to talk to me about horses. He used to work with horses and he told me about racehorses while I sat stroking his dog, Crackers, who had lovely silky ears.

Sometimes, my dad took me to Southam Zoo near Daventry. I loved to go and see the animals. Times were very different then and as a little girl, I didn't notice the small cages and poor conditions or understand that this wasn't the way that animals should be kept. I just saw the animals and I liked being able to get quite close to some of them. I don't remember too much detail – there were a number of big cats and I remember watching cubs being bottle-fed. I think there may even have been a bear cub, but perhaps I imagined that. There was certainly a chimp, and a rather random assortment of other animals; I seem to remember a fox and I think there were farm animals too. My mum took me to Wellingborough Zoo several times. I enjoyed seeing the animals but my mum didn't like going to the zoo because she said that it was cruel to keep wild animals in such cramped conditions. The cages were small and shabby and I remember it being rather smelly. The zoo closed down a few years later and I hope the animals found better homes.

Often, my dad just took me to the park on his day off. I was always happy to walk in the park, to play on the swings and to enjoy the luxury of time with my dad. I think he tried to make the time we had together as special as possible so if there was a circus or a funfair in town, he would take me to see it. I liked funfairs, especially the rides with cars, buses or fire engines that went round and round, because I liked to pretend that I was driving. I also liked candy floss, which, in those days, was only available at the fair. It was not sold in a bag as it is these days, it was made while you waited and it almost seemed like magic as the stick was wound around the candy floss maker to collect the fluffy pink candyfloss. You had to eat it quickly, before it became too sticky to cope with and it was almost impossible to manage without getting into a mess. Often, the circus people would come to the shop to ask us to display their posters in the window and they would leave a couple of free tickets in exchange. My dad liked to help them because he said they worked very hard to earn a living and when I was about three or four he got tickets to take me to the circus on his day off. I was looking forward to it because I wanted to see all the animals. I feel sure that the circus was on the Racecourse, but perhaps my memory is playing tricks on me because most of the circuses that I attended during my childhood were on Midsummer Meadow. It was very exciting, and there was music playing as we went in and found our seats, which were close to the front. The smell of animals, grass and clean sawdust were all mixed together inside the big top and we settled down to enjoy the atmosphere and watch the show. We had only watched a couple of acts when a clown came along and sat down next to me – I was absolutely terrified. I knew all about circus animals, and I don't think I would have given it a second thought if I'd found myself sitting next to a lion, but I had not encountered clowns before and I cried uncontrollably. The clown was very apologetic, but I was so upset that my dad had to take me home. My irrational fear of clowns continued for several years but I grew out of it eventually and I enjoyed other happier outings to the circus.

My parents took occasional days out instead of holidays, and on one of those days, my father took me to London. I cried when he said that we would go to Buckingham Palace to see the Queen because I thought she would be very scary, but he was teasing me. We went to Battersea Funfair and I had a lovely day. Two things stick in my mind

Me at Battersea
Fun Fair.

about the day: I had my photograph taken holding three little monkeys and I made a vinyl record for my mum. When I look at the photograph now, I have mixed feelings; it is a lovely reminder of a happy day with my dad, but I cringe to think that we treated animals so badly in those days. Making the record was great fun; we had to go into a little booth and once we had paid and pressed the button to start the process I had to sing or say whatever I wanted to be recorded. I sang a nursery rhyme and then recorded a message for my mum – I was so proud when I gave it to her. It was fun to listen to it being played on my dad's record player and to laugh at me whispering to my dad asking what to say next. I had other days out in London with my father: we visited the Tower of London, Downing Street and London Zoo. When I was five, some friends of my parents asked us to go on holiday with them to Bournemouth. My parents couldn't both go so my mum and I went, leaving my dad to take care of the shop. It was my first experience of a seaside holiday and one of the very few occasions that I stayed in a hotel during my childhood. It wasn't the warmest weather, but I enjoyed the beach and we had a nice time. The memory that sticks in my mind from that holiday is having a ride on a mechanical elephant called Simba, but I can't remember exactly where it was.

As far as I was concerned, spending time at our cottage, which was about 30 miles away in the north of the county, was better than any other outing or holiday. On Sunday afternoons, the car would be packed with food and toys and all the essentials

The cottage.

for an enjoyable afternoon. As soon as my parents finished their work in the shop we set off in the car towards Kettering. We usually listened to the radio in the car. Jimmy Clithero was a great favourite of mine and his series, *The Clithero Kid*, was often on as we travelled. I still recall the whooshing noise of passing cars as we travelled along with the car windows open. The journey of around an hour took us through Kettering and out towards Corby, past the huge cranes and the quarries that scarred the landscape, until we reached the village of Weldon. It was our routine to stop at a little shop there to buy an ice cream and I was usually allowed to buy some penny sweets; my parents didn't sell such things and, to me, they were a great treat. The last part of our journey took us towards Oundle. We drove into a pretty rural world completely different from our everyday surroundings and I loved it. The bumpy farm track led us through a field of cattle, who surrounded the car and followed us lazily across the field to the cattle grid at the top. Then we drove away from the cattle, along a lane bordered by the forest on one side and a field on the other side, variously with wheat, barley or fodder crops. The lane turned at the next cattle grid and led us past the farmhouse, on down a hill and up again towards the cottage and freedom.

For me, the afternoon stretched into endless adventure, but for my mother and grandmother there was still work to do. We often had a cooked Sunday lunch; perhaps

Uncle with some cattle.

we had cold meat, I don't recall, but the smell of minted new potatoes still conjures up memories of summer Sundays at the cottage. We always had a glass of pop with lunch on Sundays, either Tizer or my favourite, Cherryade. On other days, we drank water with meals. The farmer and his wife had become close family friends; to me they were Aunt and Uncle, and I loved them dearly. Sometimes we would go for a walk with them in the afternoon and Uncle would take me to the farmyard to see the young turkeys, or to the henhouse to help him collect the eggs. They had two dogs: Ricky, who was an outdoor dog, and Kimmy, who lived in the house. Uncle didn't like me to fuss Ricky too much because he was a working dog, but Kimmy was my friend and he followed me around when I was with Auntie and Uncle. I knew that I must never go near any of the farm machinery unless I was with Uncle, but I liked to watch the harvest from a safe distance. Usually, everyone was very busy and they hardly had time to stop for lunch, but very occasionally Uncle would let me sit on his knee on the tractor or stand in the trailer to watch the grain being transferred from the combine. Once or twice, when the combine was still and quiet, I was allowed to get up into the cab to see what it was like, but otherwise I had to stay well away from the farm vehicles.

Auntie and Uncle often took me to see bird's nests in the hedgerows or in the farm buildings. Every year, blue tits nested in some breeze blocks, which stood against the

Me at the cottage, June 1963.

wall between the house and the orchard. We couldn't look too often as it would scare the parents away, but once in a while, under the close supervision of Auntie or Uncle, I was allowed a quick peek at the eggs or at the baby birds with their beaks wide open ready for food. Very occasionally, when we walked in the forest or when we drove along the farm track, we would catch a fleeting glimpse of deer before they vanished into the undergrowth again. I always hoped for a clearer sighting, but they were shy and always alert for danger, so they spotted us long before we saw them.

Auntie and Uncle were always invited to tea when we went to the cottage. We usually had a salad with tinned salmon, pork pie or cold meat, and piles of bread and butter. Grandma always peeled the cucumber, sliced it thinly and served it in vinegar; I could eat it in those days, but I decided long ago that life was too short to wrestle with the evils of cucumber or Brussels sprouts. Throughout my childhood, tea was taken in cups with saucers. The mere mention of a mug would send Grandma into a decline and, according to her, drinking out of such a thing was like walking outside the house in your slippers – evidence of being 'common' and not properly brought up. Tea was made with loose tea in a teapot, the little spoon inside the tea caddy measuring out just the right amount of tea, one spoon for each person and one for the pot. Even on a warm summer Sunday, the teapot was adorned with a thick tea cosy to preserve the temperature while the tea brewed. There was always a homemade cake for Sunday teatime: Madeira, perhaps, or a fruit cake with almonds on the top, or my absolute favourite, cherry cake. Often there would be jelly and tinned fruit with cream as well. Tinned mandarin oranges were a special favourite of mine, but I liked them just as they were, not with cream, ice cream or anything else. My other grandmother, known to her grandchildren as Nanny, used to get the tinned oranges especially for me, but she always put Ideal milk on them – apparently my older cousin, Calvin, loved it, but I wished that she would keep it for him because it spoiled my oranges.

I had a sandpit at the cottage and a beautiful swing made by Uncle. Later on, he made me a lovely roundabout using old car seats, I had so much fun playing on the swing and the roundabout. Sometimes we took my paddling pool, my doll's pram or my little tricycle, but I was just as happy to play on my own, wandering in the lane looking for wild rabbits or bird's nests. Often, there were cattle in the field at the back of the cottage and I would spend ages leaning over the fence feeding them handfuls of long grass and letting them lick my fingers. I wasn't afraid, and even as a very tiny child I loved the cattle. There was ample evidence of the presence of moles and it was my job to jump on the molehills to flatten the soil. I only saw a live mole once; it had fallen into the pit of the cattle grid and become trapped. I wanted to stroke it until Uncle said that it would bite me, but as an act of kindness to me he rescued the mole and set it free. That is one of the few occasions that I recall him making a concession to sentiment.

Rhubarb grew in the cottage garden. Sometimes my mum would cut a nice stick of rhubarb for me, and when it was washed and cleaned, she would give me a saucer with a little bit of sugar on it to dip my stick of rhubarb and eat it raw. We picked gooseberries from the bush in the garden; I wasn't quite as keen on eating those raw, and I wasn't over fond of them cooked either! Plums from the tree in the farmhouse orchard

Tea at the cottage with Auntie, Uncle and Grandma.

were much more to my taste, as were the blackberries that grew in the hedgerows as summer turned to autumn. Uncle grew peas, potatoes, runner beans and all sorts of salad crops in the cottage garden and we often went home laden with produce. I liked to pop the pea pods and scrape the peas in to a colander, but it was a pleasure tinged with fear because occasionally the pod would contain a wriggly maggot and I dreaded accidentally touching one.

I recall very little about the homeward journey. I always looked out for the Teddy Boys in their bright suits with drainpipe trousers as we drove through Kettering, but the movement of the car soothed me to sleep long before we got home.

When I was four, Auntie and Uncle asked if I would like to stay with them for a week at the farmhouse during the summer holidays. My parents were cautious because I was so young but I was very keen to stay so they agreed, thinking that they could easily come back to fetch me if I felt homesick. To their surprise, I didn't cry and I didn't feel

Me at the farm with Uncle and his grandson, Nigel – I wanted to be in the driving seat!

homesick, and when the week drew to a close I begged them to let me stay for another week. I stayed with them every summer after that until I was in my mid-teens. I loved spending time with them and I liked the farmhouse very much. They always used the back door so that muddy boots could be left in the porch. The heavy back door had a cast-iron thumb latch rather than a doorknob and some of the internal doors had similar latches. As you walked into the back door, there was the door to the dining room on your right and the pantry door was on the left. The dining room was beautiful, but I don't recall it ever being used, even for special meals, because the kitchen, with its big farmhouse table and lovely old Aga, was so much warmer and more welcoming than the more formal dining room. The pantry was always cold. It was as big as a room with a door at either end and thick, stone shelves, which were nearly as wide as tables on either side. The other door of the pantry led into the scullery, where there was a big, old-fashioned Belfast-type sink; the washing up was done in here and much of the messier food preparation, such as skinning rabbits and preparing poultry. I watched Auntie skin rabbits several times when I was little, but then the horrible disease of myxomatosis devastated the rabbit population and, even if a healthy rabbit could be found, people didn't want to eat rabbit any more.

As you walked further into the hall, the door to the kitchen was on the left and then the hall narrowed alongside the stairs. The front door was at the opposite end of the hall and the door to the lounge was off to the right, close to the foot of the stairs. The front room had a bay window, and was big and comfortable, with a piano against the far wall. Auntie taught me to pick out a few tunes with one finger, but when it came to music, I was a very slow learner. There were three bedrooms and a bathroom upstairs. I stayed in the room over the lounge, which had two windows: a big window that looked over the field in front of the farmhouse and a little side window, which looked along the lane towards the cottage. When I woke up in the morning I liked to look out of the little window to watch the world waking up. Sometimes I saw rabbits on the grass verge near the farm track, and occasionally I saw a hare quietly nibbling a plant at the edge of the field, but if a sound or movement disturbed it, it would leap in the air and run for cover at lightning speed. I often saw pheasants pecking in the dust of the farm track and then they would vanish into the undergrowth of the hedgerow. The bathroom always had a lovely, clean smell of soap. Auntie used Fairy soap, which was a light green colour, and I still love the smell of it. Running a bath was a very slow process because the farm did not have mains water. There was a pump house in the middle of the field and once a week Uncle had to walk across the field to restart the motor of the pump. I was allowed to go with him sometimes, as long as I promised not to get too close to the motor.

I found it interesting staying with Auntie and Uncle because their daily life was very different to my own home life. At home, washing was done throughout the week as necessary, but at the farm the washing was done on a Monday and the whole day was taken up with washing, drying and ironing. The day began early with uncle fetching the water to fill the washing machine from the big rainwater tank near the hayrick; he carried the water around to the wash house one bucket at a time. They used rainwater because their pumped water was very hard and not good for use in the washing machine. The wash house was the middle of three outbuildings, which stood in a row opposite the back door of the farmhouse; it was flanked by the coal shed and the wood shed. The buildings were brick or stone built and the wash house had a window at the front with blue bags and other laundry essentials on the windowsill and a big, white sink below the window. By the time I woke up on a Monday morning, washday had already begun and the big, creamy, yellow washing machine was already chugging away. I seem to remember that Auntie had a separate boiler for some of the whites. As far as the washing machine was concerned, it was filled first and left to heat up, then the washing powder was added and it was switched to the wash setting, and a fitting at the base of the drum agitated the clothes until it was turned off again. There was no specific wash cycle, the clothes were left to wash until Auntie decided that they had been in long enough. She stayed in the wash house most of the time, keeping an eye on everything and making sure that the clothing didn't tangle in the washing machine.

She didn't mind me watching, but she didn't want me under her feet all day so she found little jobs to keep me busy. Her hens were allowed to scratch around the orchard during the day and then they were shut up in the henhouse during the evening to keep them safe from foxes. Collecting the eggs from the henhouse was one of my favourite jobs, but sometimes a hen would get broody and lay away, so when Auntie wanted a bit of peace she sent me to the orchard to look for eggs. She knew that there was plenty in the orchard to keep me busy and looking for a broody hen and missing eggs could easily take an hour or more. I hardly ever found a broody hen – probably because there wasn't one – but I had fun climbing trees, discovering caterpillars and creepy-crawlies and stroking the cattle in the field behind the orchard.

When Auntie decided that the clothes were washed, she turned off the wash function, took big wooden tongs and fished out each garment one by one. She carefully fed each item through the big mangle on top of the washing machine so that as much water as possible was removed, because this would make it much easier to rinse them. When everything from that load had been removed from the washing machine, the next load went into the same water. The day therefore started with whites and progressed through coloureds to darks and, finally, heavily soiled overalls and suchlike. It was possible to do two or even three loads before needing to change the water. I don't remember the rinse process in detail but it involved putting each item through the mangle a couple more times before anything could be hung on the long washing line in the orchard, behind the farmhouse. A dab of blue bag was added to the final rinse water for the whites. Blue bag was also used to dab on a bee sting. Auntie said it helped to take the sting away. I got several bee stings over the years because I liked to climb the plum trees in the orchard and the bees seemed to like plums almost as much as I did. The final part of washday was the ironing, which was done on the big kitchen table with two heavy irons, one heated up on the Aga while the other was being used. It was a very long job and Auntie would still be ironing in the evening.

The other routine in Auntie's week, which I enjoyed very much, was shopping day. Living on a remote farm made it impossible to buy food as needed in the way that the other adults in my life did. Auntie had to plan carefully and write a shopping list for the whole week, then on a Friday, Uncle drove us to Sainsbury's in Corby. It was my first experience of a supermarket and I was fascinated; I was able to walk around and look closely at all of the different products, which encouraged me to try new things. During my holidays at the farm, I was introduced to grapefruit (which I loved), Horlicks and Ovaltine (which were not as nice as plain milk and yoghurt). There were other things too, but I don't remember all of them. Corby was an interesting place to visit because most of the people there seemed to have strong Scottish accents. This was because a lot of people had moved from Scotland to find jobs in the steelworks at Corby.

During my stays at the farm, Auntie and Uncle always took me to visit Uncle's brother and sister-in-law on their farm near Rugby. They kept a few horses and ponies and I enjoyed being allowed to ride the ponies. I liked looking around the farm too. As far as I remember, it was mostly arable, but there was always a lot to see and do. My favourite outing during my holiday was to Wicksteed Park near Kettering. It was a wonderful place, with the biggest and most wonderful playground that I had ever

Wicksteed Park.

encountered. As well as all the usual swings, slides, seesaws and roundabouts, there were rides that you had to pay for. My favourite was the helter-skelter; if it had been left to me, I would have spent all day long trudging up the steps and sliding down the twisty slide on my mat, but my time on the helter-skelter was rationed because there were lots of other things to see and do. There was a train that took passengers for a ride around the park to enjoy the beautiful grounds. The journey took you through a tunnel and along the edge of the lake, before crossing a narrow bridge over the water and heading back towards the station. I enjoyed rides on the train and I liked looking at the water birds and other wildlife as we passed by, but I was a bit scared of the narrow bridge over the water in case I fell in. There was an outdoor fun pool and a boating lake with rowing boats and little paddle boats, which were worked by turning handles on either side, but I preferred to keep my feet firmly on dry land. Further on there was a very popular ride called the water chute. It was a boat that was on a pulley system. About a dozen passengers could be seated in the boat and then it sped down a steep ramp into the water below, causing a huge splash and soaking the passengers. The boat was then dragged back to the top to shoot down the ramp again, ensuring that anyone who escaped the water the first time got soaked on the second attempt. I was more interested in the animal area, which was housed in some buildings near the boating lake. It sounds too grand to call it a zoo, but it was rather more than a pet's corner and I absolutely loved it. I had to be enticed away with the promise that we could go back again later in the day. We usually took a picnic with us and we would go back and spread a rug on the grass by the car to sit and eat our sandwiches. We usually stayed all day but I never ran out of things to see and do.

Uncle had a grey car, which I think was an Austin Cambridge. He took good care of it and the seats, which were red, always had a lovely smell of leather and polish. In those days, seat belts hadn't even been thought about and on the way home after a busy day, I would lie on the back seat with a cover over me and fall asleep. I became fond of a number of cars as I was growing up, but I liked that one best of all; even now, the smell of leather car seats brings happy memories of outings with Auntie and Uncle flooding back. My parents' Chrysler gave up the ghost in spectacular fashion on the M1 when I was out with my dad one day. There was a burning smell and when my dad pulled over onto the hard shoulder and lifted the bonnet, plumes of smoke rose up from the engine. After that, he had a maroon Mercedes, which was nice but a bit temperamental. The car suited his needs quite well and, over time, we had a white one and then a blue one. My mum had a blue Mini, which was nice, but not terribly practical, because it didn't hold the road very well on blustery days. After that, she had a white Volkswagen Beetle, which she loved; it certainly had more room than the Mini, but it was very noisy and I was not especially fond of it.

After my father's illness, there were occasional family outings and holidays, because the doctors advised that my father should get away from the worry of the business as much as possible. In reality, it involved even more worry for my mum, because it was very hard and very expensive to get good, trustworthy and reliable cover for the shop, but it was nice for me to enjoy time with my parents. I remember the excitement of packing everything into the car, ready to go on holiday. We would leave very early in the morning, and my mum would give me a large paper bag with a selection of items to keep me occupied on the long journey. It would include a few sweets, crayons and a drawing book, a pack of Letraset Action Transfers and a selection of comics, including holiday special editions of my favourite comics. I had plenty of time to draw pictures, read my comics and set out all the Letraset transfers on the background picture by rubbing over each transfer with a ball-point pen, because it took forever to get there. Most of our holidays were in Devon or Cornwall and in the days before the motorways to the South West were built, it was necessary to plan the journey carefully before setting off, navigating from place to place along our route. I can't remember the details of the route we took, but I know that we headed for Devizes, then on towards Frome and then, some way after that, we saw a white horse cut into a hillside. We also passed what looked like an oddly shaped hill, but my dad told me that it was a Saxon burial barrow. I liked to hear his stories about Stonehenge and other ancient features of the landscape. We passed some standing stones on our journey, but I don't remember where they were. We had several holidays at a house near Stoke Fleming in Devon, which belonged to a friend of the family. I loved it there and I enjoyed my dad's stories about staying there as a boy. The nearest beach was called Blackpool Sands, which was beautiful but more shingle than sand. My dad told me that when he was young, there was beautiful sand on the beach, but some very bad storms and high tides had washed it away, leaving shingle instead. He told me that one day the sea would bring the sand

On holiday in Bournemouth in 1967 – my first seaside holiday.

back again. I'd have happily spent every day on the beach, but my parents had other ideas, and we visited various other places, including Dartmouth and Paignton. We had to cross the River Dart on the little car ferry to get to Paington; it was only a short journey but I found it rather scary because I was afraid that the ferry would sink. We had a holiday in Norfolk, one in Newquay and another in North Devon, but I liked the holidays near Blackpool Sands best of all.

My parents took us to see the Northampton Carnival every year. We chose a suitable spot to stand on the carnival route and waited excitedly in the crowd for the parade to reach us. It usually began with a band and then the float with the carnival queen and her attendants. Then there was lorry after lorry, all beautifully decorated and crawling along at walking pace, with people in costumes leaning over with nets and buckets to catch the big old pennies that we threw for them. People walked along at the side of the floats collecting money from the crowds and picking up the pennies that fell on the ground. There were people on bicycles, unicycles and suchlike too, and everyone involved in the carnival was dressed up. I liked to stay close to my parents because some of the costumes were a bit scary – I didn't like the people with huge papier-mâché heads. I knew there was just an ordinary person inside the costume but I still found them terrifying.

My mum usually used her half-day from the shop to go to the hairdresser's or to go shopping in town. Occasionally, she took me to the hairdresser's with her, but usually I went to visit my grandmother in Kerr Street while my mum was busy in town. The hairdresser's that my mum went to was called John London; it was above a shop in The Drapery but the entrance was in Jeyes Jetty (which was always pronounced 'jitty'). The hairdresser was called Jean and she kept me busy with little jobs, such as handing her rollers, so I didn't get bored, but I was happier to be left with my grandmother. I don't have many good memories of shopping in town with my mum because I disliked shopping for clothes, but I enjoyed going through the Emporium Arcade with her because her high-heeled shoes made a loud, echoing click-clack as we walked along. I liked the Emporium Arcade because my dad sometimes took me to the joke shop, which was upstairs. We bought flowers that squirted water, fake wounds, plastic flies, invisible ink and my absolute favourite – disappearing ink. My grandma went mad when the ink was spilled on the tablecloth and she remained angry even when it disappeared, but it made my dad giggle so much that it was worth getting a telling-off from Grandma.

Shopping for clothes was an ordeal for me because I had not inherited my mother's love of fashion. She always liked to look smart; she had some lovely outfits and she liked nothing better than to spend an afternoon visiting her favourite boutiques. Despite my parents providing me with the very best clothes and shoes, I'm ashamed to say that I was not at all grateful. I was not destined to follow in my mother's footsteps. I was more interested in comfort than fashion and even as a tiny child, I insisted on having my arms covered and I refused to remove my cardigan even on sweltering summer days. I was equally resistant to frills, bold patterns and tight garments of any kind, so shopping for clothes became a battle of wills. My mother made me try on countless garments but I refused to like anything. I hated having to try things on but my mum wanted my clothes to look just right, so sometimes it seemed as if I spent the whole afternoon in the fitting room. Her favourite shops for my clothes were Jack and Jill on the Market Square and Tweenage in Bradshaw Street. We occasionally went on shopping trips to Leicester to buy clothes too, usually just before Easter because I always had a new outfit at that time of year. Sometimes my mum would compromise and agree to buy something that I liked, but usually we bought the things that my mum liked, and if it was something that I really detested, the battle of wills continued each time she wanted me to wear it. I can remember searching for a best coat at Tweenage. I had my heart set on a cape and I had spotted a nice one in a muted red colour, but my mum was absolutely determined that I should have a proper coat in a brighter colour. She didn't like what she considered to be dowdy colours and she would often tell me, 'You can wear that when you're dead!' I think I must have tried on every possible garment in the shop that day before we came up with a compromise; I got my cape on condition that I would wear the coat that my mum had chosen as well. Occasionally, my mum took me with her when she shopped for her own clothes. I didn't mind that as much because I could just wait and watch while my mum tried on various outfits. She used to buy a lot of her clothes from a shop called Lucienne, which was next to the cinema on Abington Square. The lady who owned the shop was a friend of my parents' and she was always very kind to me when I visited the shop.

When my dad was growing up, he loved the cinema, and told me that he went to the pictures every Saturday morning. He was luckier than most because he was an only child and he had unmarried aunts who treated him almost as their own, so he could always find someone to give him enough money to go to the cinema. There were a lot of cinemas in the town in those days, so he could always find something interesting to watch. When he left school he became a Post Office Messenger, usually referred to as a 'telegram boy', and his wages enabled him to go to the cinema two or three times a week. He often had to deliver messages to the New Theatre in Abington Street, which enabled him to meet many of the people who performed there. He made sure that he always had his autograph book with him, and as well as signing the book, they often gave him little photographs to stick in his book. He still had his autograph book and he would show me the photographs and tell me about all the different people he'd met. I felt very sad when he told me that the beautiful New Theatre Building was gone. Apparently, audiences dwindled and after struggling for survival for a number of years, it closed. It is a pity that another use could not have been found for the building, but it was not to be; it was demolished and shops now stand in its place. We only had two cinemas in the town during my childhood: the Odeon on the Market Square and the ABC on Abington Square. My dad told me that we should make the most of them because soon they would probably be gone too. I can only recall going to the Odeon a couple of times: once on my friend's birthday to see *The Aristocats* and once with my school to see a film about Sir Edmund Hillary reaching the summit of Everest. The latter was incredibly boring, but I loved *The Aristocats*. My dad took me to the ABC several times. It was difficult for him to sit through a film because he was in constant pain, but he wanted me to enjoy the experience of going to the cinema. We saw *Steptoe and Son*, *Dad's Army* and a few other films, and I have very happy memories of those outings. My dad was right – eventually both cinemas closed, but the buildings have survived. I think my dad would have approved of the new multi-screen cinemas and he would certainly have been pleasantly surprised to know that the town still has cinemas.

In 1960s, television did not dominate our lives. We turned it on to watch something that interested us and we turned it off again afterwards. To be strictly accurate, we

My dad as a Post
Office messenger
(telegram boy).

turned the television on a few minutes before we wanted to watch it because it needed
time to warm up in order to get a reasonably clear picture. My grandma liked to watch
The Golden Shot and *Candid Camera*, my mother liked the old films that were often
on television on a Sunday afternoon and we all enjoyed watching Lucille Ball in *The
Lucy Show*. My father liked to watch *The Virginian* and I enjoyed it too – I thought
Trampas was wonderful. I watched a lot of cowboy films with my dad, especially those
that starred John Wayne because he liked those films best of all.

My first introduction to television was *Watch with Mother*, which was on for
about a quarter of an hour at lunchtime. *Andy Pandy* and *The Woodentops* were my
favourites when I was very young, but then, when I was about three, *Pogles Wood* was
first shown on television and I loved it. I liked the way it managed to weave interesting

information and film of the real world into a gentle and magical story. Looking back, it was very much of its time; Mrs Pogle was known only as 'wife' and her only existence was in the kitchen preparing the next meal for her husband and son. The little me took all that at face value but, thanks to my own mum, I grew up secure in the knowledge that anything a man can do a woman can do better. According to my mum, women have a distinct advantage because we read the instructions! Other *Watch with Mother* favourites were Bizzy Lizzy and Camberwick Green – I loved Windy Miller. I also watched *Tingah and Tucker*, which was on television on Sunday afternoons. It was about two little koalas called Tingah and Tucker and all their friends; Willie Wombat was my favourite character. I was a member of the Tingah and Tucker club and I also belonged to the Tufty club. Tufty the squirrel and his friends had been created to help children learn about road safety. I remember being very excited by the announcements about the introduction of colour television programmes, I thought our television would be able to receive colour pictures and I was so disappointed when I was told that it didn't work like that and we would have to wait until we could afford to buy a colour television.

I don't remember when I first became interested in horses, but from a very young age I had wanted to learn to ride. When I was about seven or eight, I began weekly riding lessons at Brampton Stables and I loved it. Our journey to my riding lessons took us over the level crossing at Boughton; we often had to wait for a train to pass, which annoyed my mum because time was always tight, but I enjoyed seeing them. I used to ride an elderly skewbald pony called Muffin, who was a bit bigger than some of the other ponies, but he had a lovely nature and he gave me a lot of confidence. As I progressed, I rode other ponies. A rather cantankerous mare called Star was one of my favourites. She bit me on the arm one day when I tightened her girth, and even through a coat she managed to draw blood, but I forgave her. She was also responsible for my first broken toe when she stepped on my foot awkwardly, but it taught me to be more careful and to treat her with more respect in future. Sometimes, we had a lesson in the enclosed arena in the middle of the stable yard and at other times we went out on a hack, which introduced me to the beautiful countryside around Church Brampton. I enjoyed riding along Golf Lane and over the golf course to Harlestone Firs, but I preferred the rides around Hill Farm and rides that took us towards Holdenby. To me, the views around Holdenby are the most beautiful in the whole county. Sometimes, during school holidays, it was possible to take part in day rides, which gave us a chance to ride through Harlestone, past the pheasantry, through a stream and on through the woods to Nobottle. It was a beautiful ride.

When I was nine or ten, my parents bought me a pony for my birthday. They had not discussed it with me beforehand and they chose to buy one of the riding school ponies called Geme. He was not my favourite pony at the time, but he turned out to be an excellent choice, because he was nice looking, lively and full of character. He was an enjoyable ride and he loved nothing more than cantering along a bridle path or galloping over a field. Like most ponies, he had a stubborn streak and if he didn't want to come in from the field, he would lead us a merry dance, coming close and circling around us but never getting close enough to allow himself to be caught.

Sometimes it took hours to catch him. Having Geme brought me a sense of freedom and independence, and I was able to spend weekends at the stables riding him, grooming him and cleaning his tack. I loved that pony and it felt to me as if we understood each other completely. As I grew older, I was allowed to ride out alone and was able to explore all the beautiful rides around Church Brampton in my own time and at my own pace. I grew to love the area very much; riding a horse enabled me to see and hear so much more than I would have noticed on foot or in a car, and those long rides gave me plenty of time to unwind and think through any worries or problems. Eventually, I grew too big for Geme and my parents bought me a horse called William. Geme was passed to my brother but I still rode him occasionally; I loved my horse but Geme would always hold a very special place in my heart.

Opposite above: Me riding Geme, aged around thirteen.

Opposite below: Me riding William with our car in the background, early summer 1977.

Chapter Ten

Senior School

When we arrived at senior school (always known as main school), we were finally released from the dreaded hats! It was a big change for us and the school buildings felt very big and confusing. In the lower part of the school, most of our lessons had been taken in our own classroom and most lessons were taught by our class teacher. This changed when we reached main school, where we had specialist subject teachers and had to go to different classrooms for each lesson. This involved moving between several different buildings, so on wet days we arrived for our lessons looking damp and bedraggled. It was interesting getting to know the various classrooms. They were all different and they all had character. Perhaps the best loved rooms were the attic rooms and the basement classroom. There were so many reminders around us that it was impossible to ignore the history of the buildings. Sometimes I used to look up at the main building from the path next to Miss Lightburn's lawn and wonder what life was like when it was a vicarage. In the lower part of the school, there were two forms per year group, with around twenty pupils in each form, but when we got to main school, there were three forms per year group, with up to thirty pupils in each form. Our numbers were swelled by pupils from county schools who had passed their eleven-plus exam and gained a place at the school under the government direct grant scheme. Much to my relief, I had not been able to sit the eleven-plus because I lived in the borough; I don't know if the borough had already abandoned the eleven-plus or if those who passed were sent to a different school, but only county pupils came to our school.

Platform shoes were in fashion at that time and I'd had my first pair of shoes with a (very small) platform the previous year when I was a Towerfield pupil. I had a new pair of shoes for the start of the new term at main school. They had a slightly higher platform and I was very pleased with them, but I was less pleased with the rest of my uniform. My mum had made sure that I had everything I needed for school; during the holidays, we'd made our usual trip to Sanderson's and I had endured the ordeal of trying on countless garments to ensure that I had sufficient room for growth. I had two new skirts, white blouses, two jumpers, a new blazer and a new winter coat. There was also an aertex shirt, wrap over skirt and a tracksuit for PE, all with neatly sewn name tags. At the time, I had no idea how expensive the uniform would have been or

The school grounds looking towards Becket's Park. (*Copyright Kate Baucherel*)

how much time it must have taken my mum to sew all those name tags into my clothes and I must have seemed so ungrateful. When the term started, one of the new girls, called Sally, had a lovely fashionable skirt with a hemline a couple of inches below the knee. I longed to have a skirt like hers, but I knew that it would be ages before I grew out of my new skirts. I had to wait a whole year before I was allowed to buy a more fashionable skirt for school.

As well as the new items of uniform, my kit list included a hockey stick, hockey boots and a tennis racket (with cover and press), so after our trip to Sanderson's we went to Collins Sports shop in Gold Street to buy the sports equipment. I wonder if my mum knew what a waste of money it would prove to be. I was absolutely useless at tennis and I detested hockey. There was one other item of essential equipment that we had to buy: a slide rule for maths lessons. It was very well made and it came in a rigid plastic case. I liked maths a lot better than sport and I became quite fond of my slide rule.

Each morning we would enter the school through the big, blue double gates on Derngate and walk down the ramp into the cloakrooms, which seemed to be under the school. Mr Powell, who taught biology, was my Upper Third teacher, and I liked him. Our classroom was the Biology Lab at the top of the science block, which was a modern building on the Albion Place side of the school grounds. At the back of the room, there were glass-fronted cabinets with assorted specimens preserved in jars. We got plenty of exercise going up and down stairs, and walking to and from the various school buildings for our lessons, but it wasn't a hardship – we just got on with it. We had so much to learn: there were stairs for going up and not down and vice versa; there were doors that we were not allowed to use and there was a lawn that we were forbidden to walk on, but we soon settled in and got used to the school routines.

Like most pupils, I was afraid of Miss Lightburn, our headmistress, and in awe of her deputy, Miss Harrison. There were one or two teachers that I didn't like very much, but I can honestly say that I only remember one teacher being unkind and unfair, and she didn't last very long. Miss Harrison taught me biology further up the school and I enjoyed her lessons very much, but she didn't tolerate foolishness. I remember that we were expected to dissect a worm during one lesson. I did not think it would bother me because we had previously observed the dissection of a dogfish, a frog and a sheep's eye, but this time we had to do the dissection ourselves. I had not anticipated that I would

Me (*second left*) in the school grounds close to Albion Place.

be presented with a live worm and I just couldn't bring myself to kill it by dropping it into boiling water. Miss Harrison said that she had never heard such nonsense, she took the worm and dropped it into the boiling water and then she presented me with the corpse and instructed me to get on with my work.

We had prayers every morning in the assembly hall, which was a very formal event. When we had all filed into the hall, Miss Lightburn entered through the glass doors at the back of the hall and walked briskly to the stage with the head girl trotting along behind her. We usually began with a hymn. My favourites were 'O Jesus, I Have Promised' and 'When a Knight on His Spurs in the Stories of Old'. After the hymn, there would be a Bible reading, a few words from Miss Lightburn and a prayer. At that point, the glass doors at the back would be opened and the latecomers would file in (trying not to notice Miss Lightburn's disapproving stare) before the notices were read. Lateness was frowned upon but, with so many girls travelling long distances to school by bus and train, there were bound to be occasional delays.

The only lesson that we had with Mr Powell was biology. It was one of my favourite subjects and I enjoyed his lessons. I seem to remember that the Upper Third biology syllabus seemed a little unbalanced. We studied plants in great detail and we drew intricate diagrams naming the parts of a flower and detailing the methods of reproduction. We went on to study amphibians in similar detail and if I had been a frog I would have been in no doubt whatsoever about the process of procreation. However, the chapter on human reproduction was tucked away at the back of the textbook and it seemed as if the whole process was dealt with in just a couple of lessons towards the end of the summer term, so I knew considerably less about human reproduction than that of a frog or a flower. Perhaps I am being unfair; at least we saw a film on the birth of a baby, which, as far as I remember, was very uncomfortable to watch. Several girls left the room because the sight of blood made them feel faint, but I was more troubled by the woman's pain. The film probably served its intended purpose, because after watching it I thought it was most unlikely that I would ever want to have children.

The following year, when we moved up to the Lower Fourth, we discovered the pleasures of Latin with Mr McNicholas. He was as tall as Mr Powell was short, and he was exceptionally clever. I liked him, but I wasn't so sure about Latin. The stories about Caecilius and his family in our Latin text books didn't really interest me very much; they seemed to be mostly about slave girls, werewolves and a dog called Cerberus. It was only later that I appreciated the value of learning Latin and I wished that I had worked harder in those lessons. The Lower Forth also brought us the joys of domestic science lessons – definitely not my favourite part of the week. The domestic science room was below the art room in the Cripps Block, a modern, uninspiring building in the lower part of the school grounds near Victoria Promenade. I found domestic science lessons deeply uninspiring – it was torture to me to be so close to the art room as I would much rather have been in an art lesson. We seemed to spend a lot of time talking about cooking and writing about food rather than actually doing any cooking. When we were allowed to cook, we were forced to make things that we would never eat and never cook again. One of the first things we cooked was Eggs Mornay. My family were used to good plain food, not 'messed up stuff' as my grandmother would have called it, so when I presented

The back of No. 42 Derngate. (*Copyright J. Hendy estate*)

them with Eggs Mornay, no one wanted to eat it. I also recall making lemon curd. I have never made it again since then. Thankfully, we made choices about our O Level subjects at the end of the Lower Fourth, and I dropped my least favourite subjects, chemistry and domestic science. Oddly, I quite liked physics and biology, but I hated chemistry.

I had always enjoyed English lessons, but when I reached main school, I had mixed feelings about English because I didn't like reading out loud and we did a lot of class reading, so I always tried to remain invisible. I was never a great fan of Shakespeare but we read some good books, which made a great impression on me. My favourites included *Lark Rise*, *Great Expectations*, and *Silas Marner*. I wasn't the greatest fan of our English teacher because he managed to turn a subject that I enjoyed into a bit of an endurance test, but at least he encouraged me to use the school fiction library. During my last year at Towerfield, Miss Thornton had introduced us to science fiction and it really captured my imagination. Over the next couple of years, I read as much as I could find. John Wyndham was my favourite author. The fiction library had an interesting collection of books, I enjoyed many classics such as *Vanity Fair*, *Wuthering Heights* and *The Picture of Dorian Gray*, but the book I took out time and time again was an old volume containing the complete tales and poems of Edgar Allan Poe. When we got to the Lower Fifth, we had a different English teacher, who was quite strict but I loved her lessons, and suddenly English became a pleasure.

My Upper Fourth classroom was the geography room, a bright, airy room in the main school building. At one end of the room, there were French doors leading out to the garden and at the other end, there were windows that looked out onto Derngate. I remember that one day, I accidentally stapled my thumb during a geography lesson, but I was so afraid of Mrs Durham, our geography teacher, that I chose to suffer in silence with the staple stuck in my thumb rather than admit that I had been fiddling with my stapler during her lesson. I later found that Mrs Durham had a very kind heart, but at the time she had seemed very scary. It was during our Upper Fourth year that some of the girls began to have boyfriends and to go to discos. Looking back, I think some of the girls who had come from mixed primary schools were a lot more comfortable with boys than those of us who had attended a single sex school since we were four years old. I had no time for boys and no great interest in music, so discos did not interest me. I used to listen to the Radio One breakfast show with Noel Edmonds in the mornings before school so I was aware of pop music, and I even had a small collection of vinyl singles, but music did not play a significant part in my life. I think I just listened to Radio One to annoy my mum. I remember that the arrival of Flynn the Milkman on the breakfast show each morning was my signal to head out to catch the bus for school. When I wasn't at school, I spent most of my time riding and taking care of my horse. I couldn't understand why some of my friends found scruffy lads in smelly Afghan coats attractive. I had a keen sense of smell and those coats stank, especially if it had been raining.

My Lower Fifth year was wonderful. We had the cellar classroom. I loved that room; it was tucked away beyond our cloakrooms at the end of a gloomy corridor, and it felt almost dungeon-like in the corridor, but the classroom felt special. It was our room tucked away from the hustle and bustle of the school and no one came to bother us. Mrs Haynes was our class teacher; she taught one of the less able French groups and I made quite sure that I got into her group and stayed there, because she was a fantastic teacher. Mrs Vestergaard, who was head of French, taught me for the first two years in main school. She was a very elegant woman and I don't recall her ever shouting at us or telling us off sternly, but for some reason, I found her terrifying. I didn't enjoy being in her French group and I was much happier when I was moved into the other group. The one thing that I had enjoyed while in Mrs Vestergaard's group was learning poetry in French. We had a French speaking competition and each year group had to learn a poem in French and the best speakers from each class had to recite their poem in the hall in front of the whole school. The poem that I remember most clearly is 'Le Corbeau et le Renard' and I also have vague memories of a poem about an elephant, but I can't remember the title.

Mrs Haynes set up a drama group. It was the only extracurricular activity that I took part in during my school career because I wasn't keen on giving up my free time, but I enjoyed the drama group and I was happy to give up my time to join in. Drama played an important part in school life, and Mrs Nichol organised productions every year. They were always very good with splendid sets, produced under the watchful eye of Mr Fiddes. I didn't take part in any of the productions but when there was a production of *The Wind in the Willows*, I helped to make the masks. There were many plays, mostly Shakespeare as far as I remember, but when we were in Towerfield or the

Upper Third, our year group was involved in a production of *Alice in Wonderland*. The school hall had a big stage with a number of small rooms beneath it and stairs that were always referred to as the oubliette stairs. These led down from the hall to a door, which opened onto the school grounds behind the gym. I only got the chance to visit those rooms on rare occasions; our speech and drama examinations usually took place in one of the rooms below the stage. There was also a storage area immediately below the stage which was crammed with props and costumes. I would have loved to be allowed to explore that area.

The uniform changed slightly at the start of the Lower Fifth year, we kept our navy skirts but our ties and white shirts gave way to open-neck blue blouses worn with blue jumpers. We also had very nice winter coats. I was pleased by the change, but the blouse (which had to be bought from Sandersons) proved very challenging to wear. It had a stiff collar, which was not intended to be worn open without a tie and my short neck made matters worse, so it was a constant battle to prevent the collar from touching my ears!

I was very sad to leave Mrs Haynes and our cellar classroom, but the Upper Fifth year, spent in one of the mobile classrooms with Miss Williams, was a good experience. The mobile classrooms were fairly new and very pleasant, tucked away in the beautiful school grounds. I had known Miss Williams since kindergarten but I had not warmed to her because she was a PE teacher with a boundless enthusiasm for sport, which was incomprehensible to me. I disliked PE with a passion and I could not understand her enthusiasm for such things as tennis and athletics, which I considered to be a form of torture! When Miss Williams taught me geography, I realised that she was an excellent teacher with a genuine passion for her subject. I enjoyed her lessons and I can still remember many of the mnemonics that she taught us to help us to remember important information. When she became my form teacher, I realised that she was human – she was superb and I really enjoyed my Upper Fifth year. I did not enjoy gym and dance lessons because even in the senior part of the school, we had to wear horrible aertex blouses and navy blue knickers, which made me feel very exposed. For hockey, netball, tennis and other outdoor games we wore short wrap-over skirts. Our playing fields were at the bottom of Church Way, in Weston Favell, so we travelled there by coach for hockey in the winter months and athletics in the summer. It is hard to choose which I liked least but the worst part of all was that we had to change on the coach in order to save time – I am sure such things would not be allowed these days. Every item of clothing and PE kit had to be named with an embroidered name tape sewn on neatly, which was a very time consuming job. I don't remember this being checked at Spring Hill but further up the school, we had regular inspections to ensure that all our clothing was labelled.

It is hard to say that I had a favourite teacher, because there were a number of interesting and inspirational people at the school and I still remember many of my teachers with affection and gratitude. The unforgettable Mr Fiddes taught art; he was a very good teacher, I loved his lessons and I realise now that as well as sharing very sound advice, he taught us to think for ourselves and to have the confidence to express our own opinions. Miss Elliott-Binns, who taught divinity (and so much more!), was an amazing lady. She never shied away from difficult questions and her answers showed surprising insight and understanding. I remember Father Fred Baker, who was the school chaplain and Rector of St Edmunds church. He used to take us for very occasional lessons. I am not sure what the lessons were for, but I remember liking him very much – he told good jokes and could stand on his head. I remember Miss Smith, who taught English (and despaired of my spelling), because she introduced us to poets and authors that I still enjoy reading: John Betjeman, Ted Hughes, James Kirkup, Charles Causley, Saki, E. M. Forster, Katherine Mansfield, D. H. Lawrence and many others. Most of all, I remember Mrs Nichol, because she introduced me to a wealth of wonderful poetry, which I still remember so many years later. I cannot choose just one favourite from the many that we learnt by heart, but my favourites include 'Nicholas Nye' by Walter de la Mare, 'To Daffodils' by Robert Herrick and 'I Remember, I Remember' by Thomas Hood.

I have so many memories of school life. On Ascension Day, we all walked to All Saints church for a special service, which always included the hymn 'Praise to the Lord the Almighty the King of Creation'. Every year, I seemed to end up sitting behind a pillar! We had the Gift Service before Christmas, when we all brought toys to be donated to charity. For reasons that were never clear to me, we always sang 'O Come All Ye Faithful' in Latin. When the weather was too bad for us to go outside for games,

The school grounds, back of No. 44 Derngate in the 1970s. (*Copyright Northampton High School*)

we sometimes played French cricket in the hall, which was much better than normal games lessons. At the end of term, games lessons were abandoned in favour of games of 'shipwreck' in the gym. Another end of term ritual was cleaning our desks; we had to bring in our own polish and a duster. Perhaps my best memories are of ordinary days, sitting in the area outside the gym enjoying a hot chocolate from the drinks machine on a cold day and sitting in a shady spot in the garden on a hot summer day. In my Upper Fifth year, I enjoyed taking my turn to run the Spine and Jacket book shop at lunchtimes, under the watchful eye of Mrs Tresias. Most of all, I remember the people: inspirational teachers, the gardener who kept the grounds looking beautiful and my friends. I remember my final day in uniform very well. It was a tradition that on our final school day before exam leave, we would have our blouses signed by all our friends. My mum was as practical as ever; she didn't want a dirty shirt hanging around so she gave me a laundry marker to collect the signatures.

I saw a lot of changes during my time at the school. The starchy formality of my early years at the school was almost forgotten but the high standards were still expected of us. A couple of years after I moved to main school, it was announced that the government planned to scrap the Direct Grant funding, which meant that the future of the school hung in the balance. Schools such as ours had to choose between becoming maintained comprehensive schools within the state system or fully private schools. We felt sad about it because whatever was decided would change the school forever. I remember that there were a lot of meetings about it and eventually it was decided that the school would follow the private route and a fundraising campaign began to establish a fund from which bursaries could be awarded. The Notre Dame High School for Girls in Abington Street was faced with a similar choice, but they opted to join the state system and in due course, the school moved into a different building and became the Thomas Becket comprehensive school. Several years later, the lovely convent building was torn down; even the beautiful chapel fell victim to the bulldozers. All that remains are the crosses that mark the nuns' graves; they are tucked away in a tiny memorial area in Albert Place behind Abington Street.

During my final year, the school celebrated its centenary. There were many events and celebrations during the year including a staff production of *Maria Marten, or Murder in the Red Barn*, a service at All Saints church and an open day with activities and displays, which showed how lessons were taught in earlier years. We had a whole school photograph taken too. It was a nerve-wracking experience for all concerned because we had to perch precariously on benches and wobbly platforms, but we all survived unscathed. My favourite activity was an outing to Chester for the whole school, which took place after exams in the summer term; we travelled on a specially chartered train. I don't remember very much about Chester but the train journey was wonderful and we had a lovely day.

Derngate was a happy, friendly place. Mr Fiddes once described it as an ivory tower and, of course, he was right, but I am grateful for those years. For me, school was a safe, protected and predictable environment at a time when my home life was dominated by worry and uncertainty. A lot was expected of us but I think that was a good thing for me, I probably needed to be pushed in order to do my best, but school wasn't just about results. I did better than anyone expected in my exams but more importantly I left school with a wealth of poetry in my head, a passion for books and a love of history and art. All those things have remained with me ever since. My dad once told me that a good education was the most valuable thing he could give me because it could never be taken away from me. I didn't understand him at the time, but he was right and I am very grateful for the happy years I spent at the high school.

Chapter Eleven

Changing Times

The town had been changing throughout my life. In St James, flats had risen from the rubble of the old streets, new shops had replaced the old and even the roads had been altered, but the community seemed to take the changes in its stride and daily life continued much as before. Similar changes had taken place in other parts of the town. The area that my grandmother always referred to as The Boroughs was greatly changed, with blocks of flats emerging from the dust and debris of streets that my grandmother had once called home. On The Mounts, streets that had been family homes for generations stood empty and unloved until, at last, they were demolished, leaving a devastated wasteland which served as a makeshift car park for a number of years. Everywhere you looked there was dust, debris and disruption as roads were altered and the old made way for the new. Mostly I took the changes in my stride, but I knew that it caused my parents worry when their business was put at risk by redevelopment works and I understood the deep sadness that my grandmothers felt at the loss of areas that they loved. It seemed that their past was being obliterated and, in many cases, the deep roots of community were lost. The first thing that really troubled me personally was the redevelopment of Castle station. I was too young to know about Dr Beeching and his axe or about the electrification of the line, but I knew they were spoiling 'my' station and I didn't like it.

As a result of the 1965 New Towns Act, Northampton was designated a 'new town' and in 1968 the Northampton Development Corporation was formed to redevelop the town in partnership with the local council. Much of the expansion was planned for the east and south of the town and in about 1970, work began on the eastern development. I first became aware of the plans when the parents of some of my friends began to talk about moving away from the area because they did not want to be 'swamped' by new estates. I had a school friend who lived in a nice house at Orchard Hill, Little Billing; I used to go to her house for lunch on my half-day from school before we both went riding. When you drove out along the Wellingborough Road before the redevelopment, there was very little in the way of buildings beyond Booth Lane and when we drove to my friend's house in Little Billing, it felt like driving through the countryside. I can understand why they moved away- they thought that they would be swallowed up by the redevelopment and if they had stayed they would have had to endure years of disruption as the new estates were built. Like many people in the town, my parents were not overjoyed about having large numbers of people, who were always referred to as 'London overspill', relocated to the town. People felt that so many newcomers with London accents would cause our own local accent to be changed beyond recognition and, to some extent, they were right, but accents change over time anyway. I think people of my mum's generation and older remembered the difficulties when a lot of people from London were sent to the town as evacuees during the Second World War. This was different because the people who came wanted to be here and wanted to become part of the community. Locals looked at the new developments and saw a stark ugly landscape of houses like little boxes; to us, it was a blot on a once beautiful landscape, but the newcomers saw it very differently, they saw potential and opportunity.

Our first experience of the eastern district was on our journeys out towards Kettering, on the way to our cottage. Roundabouts sprang up and the landscape, which had been so familiar to us, was suddenly barren and bewildering, and we felt like strangers in our own town. I remember going to have a look at Weston Favell Centre with my parents soon after it opened in 1974 – they were not very impressed. I'm not sure what they expected but I remember that it felt very drab and unwelcoming. I think my

Looking up the Drapery. Boots can be seen on the left before its move to the Grosvenor Centre.

parents were overwhelmed by the ugliness of the building; it took several years before the newly planted shrubs and trees became established and softened its appearance. I seem to remember that Tesco at Weston Favell Centre was the largest single-storey supermarket in Europe at that time, but it didn't impress my parents and they never went back. I did not visit the centre again until the early 1980s. By then, I had friends who lived in the eastern district and I realised that it was a pleasant place to live with lots of open space and safe places for the children to play.

There were so many changes taking place around the town centre that it is hard to remember what happened when. In 1972, or thereabouts, a tall grey-and-white hotel, which looked as if it had a white frill around the top, emerged from the wreckage of Horsemarket to overshadow the churchyard where St Katherine's church had once stood. It was known at that time as the Saxon Inn, but it has had several names (and colours) since then. At much the same time, the new Barclaycard building opened on Marefair. I disliked it because it seemed huge and ugly and certainly not in keeping with its surroundings but, looking back at old photographs, I have to confess that it wasn't really that bad. Nevertheless, I'm glad it's gone. Northampton House, an ugly twelve-storey blot on the landscape, was built in 1973 and the whole community seemed united in their disapproval of the building, which was deeply disliked. It began life as council offices, but it was later converted into flats.

I felt sad when the United Counties bus station in Derngate closed because it had been a familiar part of my life for as long as I could remember and I was quite fond of the building. Like many of the pupils at my school, I was also fond of Robertson's sweet shop, which was close to the bus station. It was only a small shop, but it managed to cope with the sea of school girls that swept along Derngate on their way to the bus station at the end of the school day. My parents had their own business and I knew enough about passing trade to realise that the closure of the bus station would mean that the sweet shop suffered a significant loss of custom, which could threaten its survival. I liked the new Greyfriars bus station, which opened in 1976. A lot of people complained that the building, which had offices and a car park above it, was hideous and I have to admit that it was not a thing of great beauty, but they were building a bus station not a cathedral. With the benefit of hindsight, I can see that there were some mistakes made in terms of planning, which led to problems accessing the bus station when the shopping centre was closed. However, I saw it as a great improvement on the bus stops that had previously been scattered around the town centre streets. In comparison, it was warm, dry and convenient.

I liked the new Grosvenor Centre too. It seemed to me that the town had been a building site for years, but when it opened, we were rewarded with a selection of new shops as well as some familiar stores that had relocated to the new centre. Boots moved into a smart new store, but I felt rather sad to see their old premises on the corner of the Drapery standing empty. Chelsea Girl quickly became my favourite place to shop because, at long last, I had been given the freedom to choose some of my own clothes. My mother despaired when I chose garments in dark blues and browns with skirts that were several inches below my knees, but her protests fell on deaf ears. Beatties was interesting; I liked their haberdashery department very much and they

The Grosvenor Centre.

sold beautiful china too, but I had to hold my breath on the way in because the smells from the cosmetics department were overpowering. I loved to look around Habitat to choose things that I would buy for my bedroom if I could afford it. I liked Taylor and McKenna too. I was too old to be very interested in the toys but I liked the balsa wood and all the modelling materials for railway layouts and suchlike. My brother had a rather nice model railway layout and I used to take him to Marks, in the Drapery, to buy engines, rolling stock and accessories. There were always lovely smells from the baker's, which I think was called The Oven Door.

The town paid a very high price for our smart new shopping centre. We lost the beautiful but rather down-at-heel Emporium Arcade. When I see how other towns have restored and preserved their old arcades, I can't help feeling that the decision to demolish the Emporium Arcade was extremely short-sighted. I wish I could say that we have learnt from the mistakes of the past, but, sadly, other important buildings have been lost. I know that the town has to adapt and develop in order to meet the changing needs of the community, but we must value and preserve the best from the past as well as building for the future. We could all speak with sadness and regret about buildings that have been lost. For my mum, it would probably be Prince's Street Baptist church, which played such an important part in her life as she was growing up. For many, it would be the Notre Dame High School and convent in Abington Street, which was torn down before anyone had time to object. I regret the loss of St Edmund's church and, though it may sound trivial in comparison, I also regret the loss of our station buildings and so much of the railway infrastructure that I took for granted as a child.

The early 1970s brought disruption and change to my home life too. The journey to and from the shop became increasingly difficult for my parents to cope with. The redevelopment of the town centre, and other areas including Grafton Street and St James, caused a lot of traffic problems. It had once been a problem-free drive of no more than fifteen minutes, but it became a stressful and tedious crawl that could take almost an hour. I think my mum felt that she was always racing against the clock in order to fulfil her responsibilities. My brother and I were happy and well looked after by our grandmother, but I remember the long waits for our parents to come home. I clearly remember the interminable wait for them to come home on Christmas Eve; we were so excited, but it seemed as if Christmas couldn't begin until they got home. Poor Mum – she worked so hard, but it was impossible for her to be in two places at once.

My grandma died when I was twelve and my little brother was five. It came as a big shock to me because she had not shown any sign of illness. She had seen the doctor for what she thought was a fairly trivial problem, but tests revealed that she had a

Abington Street, with Notre Dame High School on the right.

cancerous tumour and she was told that she needed surgery. She went into hospital for the operation a few days before Christmas. The procedure was carried out successfully, but she died shortly afterwards. Perhaps it was better that way. At least she was spared further suffering; I think she had decided that she was ready to die. I felt her loss deeply. I missed her so much and it took me a long time to adjust to life without her. I wasn't blind to her faults, but she was a good grandmother and I loved her very much. Despite her old-fashioned ways, she had let me do things that my parents would never have permitted such as staying up late to watch television with her when she babysat for us on a Friday evening. Sometimes we watched a thriller and afterwards I was too scared to go up to bed on my own.

After my grandmother's death, things became increasingly difficult for my mother. She had to be at home to take care of us and to prepare meals but she was needed at the shop too because my father was still in poor health. It became clear that something had to change and my father began to talk about the possibility of moving back to the shop. I welcomed the idea because I had been happy there and it seemed a sensible solution to the problem, but my mum loved living in Weston Favell and she was reluctant to move. We remained at Hillside Way for two or three years after my grandmother's death, but in the end my mum agreed that moving back to St James was the only sensible option. So in due course the house was sold and we left Weston Favell behind to move back to the flat above the shop. My brother seemed sad to leave his friends behind and my mum had a very heavy heart, but I had no regrets – I was pleased that the move would make life a little easier.

We soon adapted to our new routine. There was still plenty of rushing about for my mum to do because she had to take my brother to school and collect him at the end of the day. This meant that I usually got a lift to school too, but I went home on the bus. My maternal grandmother had become frail and she moved from Abington to a warden-supported ground-floor flat in Portland Place, close to Abington Square. My mum and my aunts did their best to support her and one or other of them called in on her every day, but it wasn't enough. She had several episodes where she lost track of time and seemed very confused, and it became clear that she could no longer live on her own. No one wanted her to go into a home and my mum wanted her to come and live with us, but it was impossible. It broke my mum's heart when she had to admit that she couldn't give my grandmother the care that she needed as well as coping with everything else. She was offered a place in a nice home in Cotswold Avenue and her daughters visited her every day. Sadly, she became increasingly confused and she often seemed unsettled and anxious, but she was well cared for and treated kindly by the staff.

I sat my O Levels in May 1978 and then a whole summer of freedom stretched ahead of me. September would come all too soon, bringing with it new experiences and new challenges, but I wasn't looking that far ahead – I was going to enjoy the summer. All of my free time was spent at the stables and I remember that summer with great affection. One day, towards the beginning of August, I was called into the office to take a phone call from my mum; she sounded anxious and she asked me to come home as quickly as I could because my father was unwell and the doctor had arranged for him to be admitted to hospital. She needed me to work in the shop while she went to the hospital with my dad. I was standing at the counter serving a customer when my dad came downstairs and walked behind me on his way out of the shop. He spoke to me and ran his hand across my shoulders as he went past but I hardly had time to acknowledge him because I was busy with a customer. That was the last time I saw him. He suffered a cerebral haemorrhage, which was so severe that he had no hope of survival. They said that he would survive for no more than forty-eight hours, but he proved them wrong. He survived for a month, unable to move or respond, but perhaps able to hear. My mum stayed with him day and night, she popped home briefly each day to wash and change her clothes and to check on me and my brother. I took care of my brother and did my best to keep the shop running smoothly so that my mum was free to focus on my dad. After a couple of weeks, my brother went to stay with his friend, which was better for him and one less thing for my mum to worry about. My dad died on 8 September 1978. He was fifty-two.

During the month that my dad was in hospital, I realised that my plans for September would have to be put on hold because my mum would need my help for the next few months. We were grateful for so many acts of kindness but the one that meant a great deal to me personally took place a few days after my father's death. Miss Lightburn telephoned to offer her condolences to my mum and to speak to me. I had spent my school life doing my best to remain invisible and I had never had any personal dealings with Miss Lightburn, so I was surprised that she even knew who I was. She would have had my school record in front of her, but she also knew little things about my friends and about the thing that I enjoyed. She told me that I should be very pleased with my O Level results and I should not give up on my education. She was right, of course, and, in due course, I followed her advice, but first I needed help my mum to make plans for the future.

In earlier years, my grandmother would have been a great support to my mum, but sadly she was too confused to fully understand my mum's sadness. My aunt had done her best to explain to her that my dad had died and she had been very upset about it, but by the time she saw my mum, she had forgotten about it and my mum had to break the news to her all over again. This happened again and again, and every time it was as if she was hearing the news for the first time; it was upsetting for my mum and very upsetting for my grandmother. In the end, it was easier and kinder not to tell her, and when she asked how he was, my mum would tell her that we were all alright. My grandmother died unexpectedly in November of that year. It was a sad end for a lovely lady and I wish her last days had been happier.

1978 was a difficult year. It marked the end of my childhood and the loss of two very precious people. There was a bumpy road ahead, but as my grandmother Ethel often said, 'Whatever doesn't kill you makes you stronger.' This was the end of a chapter, but it was the start of a new one too, and I carried a wealth of love and happy memories with me on my journey through life. In time, other special people would become part of my life including my stepfather who, along with my mum, has been there for me through all the joys and sorrows of my adult life.

Acknowledgements

I am grateful to Frank Baverstock, Mary Grant and the members of the Northampton Past Community for sharing their memories and creating such a wonderful local history resource. Without their support and encouragement this book would never have been written.

I am indebted to Simon Hendy, John Evans, Kate Baucherel, Gayle Law and Northampton High School for Girls for allowing me to use their photographs in the book. Thanks also to Brenda Broome, Emily Jones, Claudia Sciumbata and Clare Jones who helped me to bring order to a tangle of memories.

ALSO AVAILABLE FROM AMBERLEY PUBLISHING

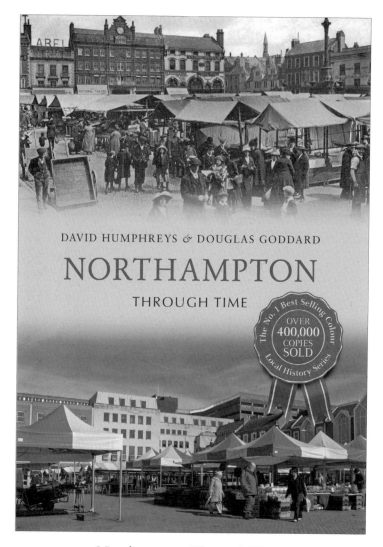

Northampton Through Time
David Humphreys & Douglas Goddard

This fascinating selection of photographs traces some of the many ways in which Northampton has changed and developed over the last century.

978 1 4456 1656 8

96 pages, full colour

Available from all good bookshops or order direct from our website www.amberley-books.com